The Go-Ahea
The First 25 Years

MARK LYONS

KEY
Books

BRITAIN'S BUSES SERIES, VOLUME 5

Front cover image: Go South Coast comprises a number of operators in southern England, each of which retains its separate identity. Solent Blue Line uses the Bluestar brand and, 1127 (HF58 KCC) is seen near Otterbourne.

Title page image: In recent years the Go-Ahead Group has acquired a number of high-quality independent bus operators in southern and eastern England. Typical of these is Konectbus, which joined the Group in March 2010. It operates park and ride services Norwich together with a range of inter-urban links centred on Norwich and its home base in Dereham, Norfolk. The latter include express service 8, which is operated using a fleet of leather-seated Enviro400 double-deckers new in early 2012. Showing off the distinctive livery carried by these vehicles is 609 (SN61 CZZ) seen in Castle Meadow, Norwich. Konectbus prides itself on the appearance of its fleet and, unusually, the lower panels of its livery are pale coloured, which helps emphasise the high standards of cleanliness.

Contents page image: Since this book was originally published in 2012, Go-Ahead Group has continued to expand in the UK and overseas. It now provides rail services in Germany and Norway along with buses in Dublin and Singapore. Go-Ahead Singapore 5101, a Wrightbus Eclipse Gemini-bodied Volvo B9TL, is seen at Changi in October 2016.

Bibliography

Bus Operators: 2 – NBC Antecedents & Formation, Stewart J. Brown, Ian Allan 1983

National Bus Company – the road to privatisation, Kevin Lane, Ian Allan 2006

The Definitive History of Wilts & Dorset Motor Services Ltd 1915-1972, Colin Morris and Andrew Waller, The Hobnob Press 2006

Wilts & Dorset 1915-1995 Eighty Years of Motor Services, Steve Chislett, Millstream Books 1995

Northern and its Subsidiaries, Keith A. Jenkinson and S. A. Staddon, Autobus 1995

A History of OK Motor Services, David Holding, Bus Enthusiast Publishing 2007

Southern Vectis 1929-2004 – 75 Years Serving the Isle of Wight, Richard Newman, Colourpoint 2004

Pride & Joy: My Amazing 25-year Journey with Brighton & Hove Buses, Roger French, Best Impressions 2010

Buses Focus 11 – Summer 1999, Gavin Booth and Stephen Morris, Ian Allan 1999

Buses Focus 38 – November-December 2005, Gavin Booth and Stephen Morris, Ian Allan 2005

All Change: British Railway Privatisation, Roger Freeman and John Shaw, McGraw Hill 2000

Periodicals

Buses, Ian Allan Ltd/Key Publishing Ltd

The London Bus, The London Omnibus Traction Society

Modern Railways, Ian Allan Ltd/Key Publishing Ltd

First published in 2012 as *The Go-Ahead Group* by Ian Allan. This edition published in 2020 by Key Books.

Key Books
An imprint of Key Publishing Ltd
PO Box 100
Stamford
Lincs PE19 1XQ

www.keypublishing.com

The right of Mark Lyons to be identified as the author of this book has been asserted in accordance with the Copyright, Designs and Patents Act 1988 Sections 77 and 78.

ISBN 978 1 913870 29 4

Typeset by SJmagic DESIGN SERVICES, India.

Contents

Introduction

The Go-Ahead Group's origins lie in the privatisation of the National Bus Company, which saw its 72 subsidiary businesses sold, in many cases to their existing management teams. One such buy-out was that of the Gateshead-based Northern General Transport Company, sold to a team comprising Martin Ballinger, Chris Moyes, Trevor Shears and Jim Weeks in 1987. Although the newly established Go-Ahead Northern concentrated initially on establishing itself in its north-eastern heartland, a process that was not without some pain, it subsequently followed a considered process of expansion, focusing mainly on urban bus operations in the south-east of England. This change of emphasis from being a regional bus operator to a Group with national ambitions was aided by a stock market flotation and prompted adoption of a new name, the now familiar Go-Ahead Group. The privatisation of London Buses and British Rail provided further opportunities for expansion; Go-Ahead is now the largest provider of bus services in London and its rail services carry more passengers than any other operator.

Whilst some of the transport groups that emerged as the industry consolidated adopted a centralised approach to management, reinforced by national liveries, Go-Ahead Group believes that public transport is essentially a local business and that what works well in one area cannot necessarily be applied somewhere else. The Group therefore allows its operating subsidiaries to manage their businesses locally, thus fostering effective relationships with local authorities and other stakeholder groups. This approach has seen Go-Ahead companies consistently at the top of most measures of success, amongst both passenger groups and industry.

In 2000, the Group was the subject of a hostile takeover bid by C3D, a subsidiary of the French government agency Caisse des Dépôts et Consignations, and Rhône Capital. Although the bidders claimed that a takeover would allow them to transform their Transdev subsidiary into a pan-European public transport business, there were suspicions that its timing was designed to destabilise negotiations then under way that would ultimately see Govia, a joint venture between the Group and SNCF, win the South Central rail franchise from French company Connex. This instability caused National Express to declare that it would consider a bid for the Group if it were to be broken up. Although C3D offered £326m for the Group, this was considered to represent an undervaluing of the business and shareholders showed their confidence in the Group's management by rejecting the bid.

Although the Group has remained focused on UK rail and bus operations, with an emphasis on urban markets in London and the south-east, it has, nevertheless, also sought to diversify its portfolio where suitable opportunities exist. This approach has seen the Group expand at different times into pubs, car park management and aviation ground and cargo handling. These non-core activities have now been disposed of as, although generally profitable, they required a disproportionate amount of management time.

Martin Ballinger retired in 2004 and was replaced by Chris Moyes, who had been Deputy Chief Executive since 1999. He was also instrumental in establishing GoSkills, the transport sector skills council, of which he was Chairman. In 2006, he was forced to retire due to ill health and, sadly, he died in September of that year. His successor as Group Chief Executive was Keith Ludeman, who had led the buy-out of London General in 1992 and been appointed to manage the Group's growing rail portfolio in 1999. Mr Ludeman retired in July 2011, to be replaced by David Brown, who had previously been the Managing Director of Surface Transport at Transport for London (TfL). He is, however, no stranger to the Group and was Chief Executive of London Central and London General between 1999 and 2006. The Group has therefore benefited from a high level of continuity at senior management level.

As it reaches its quarter-century Go-Ahead has become a £2.2bn business, carrying nearly three million passengers per day in a fleet of around 3,800 buses and 830 trains. Although the next few years will be challenging, the Group is well placed to respond and will continue to seek opportunities to grow. Although its subsidiaries will continue to be managed locally, the economies of scale that can be achieved by being part of a larger organisation, for example in vehicle and fuel purchasing, will help ensure that the Group is able to provide an attractive, value-for-money service to its customers whilst delivering a return for shareholders. The Group's approach to customer services has been vindicated through a number of passenger and industry awards and, in 2011, Passenger Focus, the independent watchdog, reported that its bus services outside London achieved a satisfaction level of 91%. The Group aims to further improve the passenger experience and, in addition to taking forward the recommendations made by the 2011 survey, has become the first major UK bus operator to commit itself to an annual independent customer satisfaction survey.

The Group continues to see impressive growth as a result of effective marketing, a continuing shift away from cars and onto buses and trains, and initiatives such as "the Key", its smartcard ticket which is being rolled out across all its operations outside of London. Although all tickets are to the same ITSO technical standard, individual operating companies have adapted it according to their local market requirements. This has seen the development of integrated pay-as-you-go smartcard ticketing between Southern, Metrobus and Brighton & Hove services, whilst Go North East has focused on developing a lifestyle-type product, delivered via a mobile-'phone app, and Oxford Bus Company has introduced an inter-operable smartcard in partnership with Stagecoach as part of the Transform Oxford programme.

Public transport plays a vital role in improving the environment and Go-Ahead plans to cut its carbon emissions per passenger journey by 20% by 2015. Regenerative braking has reduced energy consumption on its third rail fleet by 15% and hybrid buses are being introduced across the group. It is also working with Williams Hybrid Power to develop a flywheel energy storage system for buses and has fitted Telematics monitoring to over 4,000 vehicles, delivering fuel savings of around 12%. In May 2012, it was named the 10th best company in the world for its social, environmental and governance performance by EIRIS, an independent researcher into the ethical performance of companies.

Go-Ahead has grown to become one of the UK's leading providers of passenger transport, delivering bus and rail services to predominantly urban markets. Its rail services carry more passengers than any other and it is the largest provider of bus services in London. Employing around 22,000 people across the country, over one billion passenger journeys are taken on its bus and rail services each year.

In addition to developing its existing markets, the Group continues to seek opportunities for expansion both in the rail market and by seeking to acquire high-quality bus operators. It remains committed to its devolved structure and local focus to generate passenger growth, a structure that allows it to closely manage the performance of each operating company while giving local managers the autonomy they need to run their businesses. The overarching principle is to combine the value of this local identity culture with the financial benefits of Group scale and transfer of best practice.

This volume looks at the history of the companies that have come together to form the Go-Ahead Group from its roots in the north-east of England to the major transport provider of today.

Although this is not an official publication of the Group, I would like to record my thanks to those staff and officials of the Group and its operating subsidiaries who have provided invaluable assistance in the preparation of this title. I am also grateful to the photographers who have allowed me to use their work in these pages.

2020 Update

This volume was originally published in 2012 to coincide with the Go-Ahead Group's quarter century. Since then it has continued to expand, acquiring Thamesdown Transport, East Yorkshire and the Queen's Road operations of First Manchester. It has also won contracts to operate services on behalf of Cornwall Council. Bournemouth-based Excelsior Coaches and Tom Tappin's Oxford sightseeing business have also joined the Group. Management of Metrobus' Transport for London contracted services now falls under Go-Ahead London, with the remaining services administered by Brighton & Hove. Both continue to trade under the Metrobus brand.

In 2014, Govia was awarded the UK's largest rail franchise – the Thameslink, Southern and Great Northern contract, which is running under the trading name of GTR (Govia Thameslink Railway). This, and the South Eastern operation, are currently being operated under direct contract from the Department for Transport whilst new arrangements to replace rail franchising are developed.

In 2015, Go-Ahead was awarded its first notable overseas operations. The Loyang bus tender, which commenced operations in September 2016, in Singapore comprises a network of routes in the east of the island. Further international expansion saw Go-Ahead awarded the Outer Dublin Metropolitan Area bus contract by the National Transport Authority of Ireland (NTA) with operations starting in September 2018. The Group's German subsidiary, Go-Ahead Bus and Bahn, has been awarded five rail contracts. It also operates the Oslo South rail package, the first rail contract to be let in Norway. Growth overseas was partly offset by the loss of the West Midlands rail franchise in 2017.

Recent years have seen an increased awareness of the environmental benefits of public transport. Go-Ahead London currently has the largest fleet of battery electric buses in the UK, and this technology is also in use with Go South Coast and Go North East, whilst Metrobus is planning to introduce hydrogen fuel-cell buses onto the Crawley Fastway network. Brighton & Hove has invested in extended range hybrid buses capable of running in zero emission mode in the city centre.

Chapter 1

Northern General
From subsidiary to independence

The Go-Ahead Group grew out of the north-east of England with its roots in the Northern General Transport Company, incorporated on 29 November 1913 to bring together a number of operations in the region owned by the British Electric Traction Company (BET). Established in 1896 to acquire and develop urban tramways, BET took over the Gateshead & District Tramways Company the following year.

The acquisition of Gateshead & District was swiftly followed by expansion and electrification of the network. In 1899 BET expanded further in the north-east acquiring the North Shields & District Tramway Company which, in anticipation of electrification, was renamed the Tynemouth & District Electric Tramway. In 1903 the newly formed Jarrow & District Electric Tramway come under BET control. Gateshead & District obtained powers to operate motor buses in 1909 although the first route, linking Chester-le-Street with Low Fell, was not introduced until May 1913. Rapid expansion of bus services followed and a sizeable network was established based upon Chester-le-Street, the focal point for many of the towns and villages of the Durham coalfield.

The newly created Northern General assumed control of Gateshead & District, Jarrow & District and Tynemouth & District tramways, although they retained their separate operating identities. The bus operations of Gateshead & District were vested directly in Northern General, which adopted the "Northern" fleetname and a bright red livery contrasting with the maroon trams. The bus network continued to grow, with Newcastle being served from August 1914, although expansion was halted by the outbreak of hostilities that month, which saw much of the bus fleet requisitioned to support the war effort.

Following the armistice, growth resumed and in 1921 a new depot and central workshop facility was opened at Bensham, on a site still occupied by Go North East. There was no central licensing of bus services at this stage,

The Gateshead & District Tramways fleet contained a large proportion of single-deck cars. Locally built 10 was one of a number used to modernise the network in the early 1920s and is now preserved at the Beamish Open Air Museum. (Steven Hodgson)

Northern General developed the SE6 to meet its need for a high-capacity single-decker. Although most carried bus bodywork, six, including 652, were built as coaches. When new in 1935 it had a folding sunroof, although this was replaced by a luggage rack in 1939. (Go North East)

although many local municipalities did regulate services within their areas, and many smaller operators sprang up in the heavily populated industrial areas of the region. Whilst some of these operators enjoyed a long independent existence, many ceased trading as the realities of operating bus services became apparent. In a foretaste of a policy of acquisition that has continued to this day, Northern General bought Gateshead-based Crescent Bus Company on 1 January 1924, followed in 1925 by the Invincible Motor Omnibus Company of Seaham Harbour.

By the early 1920s the bus fleet was becoming standardised on Leyland and Daimler chassis, although a number of buses based on running units built by the Birmingham & Midland Motor Omnibus Company (BMMO), better known as Midland Red, also joined the fleet. The tramway operations also benefited from investment in new rolling stock. The decade saw steady expansion, facilitated by improved road infrastructure and more reliable vehicles. In 1928 the opening of the Tyne Bridge improved access to Newcastle and a bus station was constructed at Worswick Street.

On 28 December 1929 the London & North Eastern Railway (LNER) acquired a shareholding in Northern General, prompting an agreement to co-ordinate rail and road services within the district. One of the consequences was the acquisition of the business of Wakefield's Motors, in which the LNER had purchased a stake earlier in 1929. The company, which operated a number of services mainly in and around Whitley Bay, retained its separate identity, although it was placed under the control of Tynemouth & District.

The 1930 Road Traffic Act introduced a national system of licensing for bus services under the control of the Traffic Commissioners, with the aim of bringing high and consistent standards to the industry and reducing wasteful competition. A consequence of the new regime was to freeze the operating territories of established bus operators, as any new entrants were effectively prevented from initiating services by the objections from existing operators. As a general rule, the only way in which significant expansion could be achieved was by acquisition of an existing operator and its licences.

A significant acquisition was that of the Sunderland District Transport Company, which was finally taken over after protracted negotiations in January 1931 and continued to operate as a subsidiary of Northern General. During the 1930s the tramway networks were beginning to require significant investment in track and fleet renewal, the cost of which was deemed excessive. As a result the Tynemouth & District system was closed in stages, with buses replacing trams.

Northern General's operating area was bedevilled by a large number of low bridges, which prevented operation by double-deck vehicles on what were often heavily loaded services, and as a result the company required high-capacity single-deck buses. Construction and Use regulations limited two-axle vehicles to 27 feet in length and a front-mounted engine took up valuable space that could be used by passengers. The company's Bensham works

New to Sunderland District, Tyneside 66, a Burlingham-bodied Leyland PD3, had been repainted in the dark green and cream livery of its new operator when caught on camera at Percy Main. (Ian Athey)

Northern General was an early supporter of rear-engined double-deckers. Gateshead & District 88, an Alexander-bodied Leyland Atlantean, was one of the first to join the fleet in 1959. (David Little)

had considerable engineering expertise, and accordingly in 1933 a side-engined 45-seat single-decker, with a three-axle chassis designed in conjunction with AEC and bodywork based on a Short Brothers product, was unveiled. Further examples of the type, designated SE6, followed, although most of these were built under licence by AEC. A two-axle derivative, the SE4, which seated 40 passengers, followed.

The company continued to expand by acquisition and, in 1936, the Wallsend-based operations of Tyneside Tramways & Tramroads, operating as Tyneside, were taken over. The tramway itself had been abandoned in April 1930 to be replaced by motor buses carrying a green livery.

As in 1914, the outbreak of war on 3 September 1939 put an effective halt to most developments within the Northern General fleets, which by that time numbered 666 buses and 78 tramcars. Although a few new vehicles, largely those on which construction had already started at the outbreak of hostilities, joined the fleet in 1940, large numbers of buses were once again requisitioned for the war effort. The pressure on the remaining fleet was increased by a combination of the heavy demands made by essential workers employed in supporting the war effort and the inevitable air raids inflicted on the region. From 1942 onwards, in addition to some of its requisitioned vehicles returning, the company began to receive new vehicles built on Guy Arab chassis with bodywork to the Ministry of Supply's austerity standard. The seating layout in many single-decker buses was altered to longitudinal benches which allowed up to 30 standing passengers to be carried and, in a bid to save oil, a number of vehicles were converted to run on producer gas, produced from coal in a small trailer towed behind the bus.

The return of peace in 1945 was accompanied by a desire to return to normal as quickly as possible. New buses were ordered, these being built on Guy and AEC chassis to initiate fleet renewal. The pace of new deliveries was very slow and a number of vehicles were heavily rebuilt as a short-term measure.

Although BET successfully opposed nationalisation of its bus-operating businesses by the Labour government elected in 1945, the State did gain some control through acquisition of the shares previously held by the railways, including the LNER's stake in Northern General.

By the late 1940s the need to renew the Gateshead & District tramway fleet, the last operated by a BET company, was becoming pressing. Although pre-war plans had envisaged replacement of the fleet with trolleybuses, and legislation to enable this was in place, the decision was taken to use diesel-powered buses instead. The Gateshead & District Tramways Act 1950, enabling the conversion to take effect, became law on 12 July 1950, whereupon the company changed its name to Gateshead & District Omnibus Company Ltd. The last trams were withdrawn from service on 4 August 1951, having been replaced by a fleet of new Guy Arab and Leyland Titan double-deckers.

The company continued to expand during the 1950s, both through acquisition of existing operators, such as J. W. Hurst & Son of Winlaton, which was taken over in August 1951, and by introducing routes to serve new housing estates being built to replace sub-standard housing in the region.

Venture was acquired by the National Bus Company in 1970 and placed under Northern General's control, although the fleet retained its separate identity until 1974. 218, a 1960 Park Royal-bodied AEC Reliance, is seen heading towards Scotwood Road, Newcastle. (David Little)

An early sign of NBC standards was the arrival of the first ECW-bodied Bristol RE in the Northern General fleets. Northern 2839 (LCN 105K) was delivered to Gateshead & District in 1971 but quickly transferred to the Northern fleet. When photographed in Stanley in July 1973 it was carrying an NBC corporate fleetname but retained traditional Northern livery. (David Little)

Most notable, however, was the delivery in 1963 of the first of 50 front-entrance AEC Routemasters with Leyland engines for use on long-distance services. In an echo of the concerns being expressed today about the impact of vehicle weight on fuel economy it was reported that the Routemaster's lightweight construction made it more fuel-efficient than the heavier Atlantean and Fleetline models. In 1966 a 51st Routemaster, London Transport's RMF1254, which never operated in passenger service with LT, joined the indigenous fleet.

Northern General's livery was simplified during the 1950s, with single-deckers outshopped in unrelieved red for a while. A more significant change saw the Gateshead & District fleet adopt a dark green and cream scheme from 1964 replacing the maroon that dated back to tramway days. Sunderland District buses remained blue, whilst those of Tynemouth & District were red.

A key transport commitment of the Labour government of 1966-70 was the establishment of an integrated transport plan in which local authorities were responsible for planning decisions and bus services, with a national bus company bringing together the operations of the already state-owned BTC and those of BET. Faced with the prospect of compulsory acquisition, the latter entered into discussions with the government and its bus-operating subsidiaries duly passed into State control as part of the newly created Transport Holding Company (THC) on 1 March 1968. Shortly afterwards the Transport Act 1968 became law and saw the establishment of the National Bus Company. This took control of the THC's bus-operating subsidiaries, including Northern General, in England and Wales with effect from 1 January 1969.

Other elements of the 1968 Act that had a significant impact on Northern General were the establishment of Passenger Transport Authorities in the major conurbations which would, through their Passenger Transport Executives, take over municipally-owned transport undertakings. Those operated by Newcastle upon Tyne and South Shields duly passed to Tyneside PTE on 1 January 1970. The Act also established a new bus grant of 25% (later increased to 50%) towards the costs of new buses that conformed to certain specifications, most notably suitability for one-person operation, and allowed for local authorities to pay subsidies for rural bus services.

The first outward manifestation of the National Bus Company in the Northern General area was the transfer of vehicles from other NBC companies, most notably a number of Bristol Lodekkas, a type not previously operated by the company; these arrived from Crosville. Other unfamiliar new types of bus included rare Daimler SRG6 single-deckers, which were then followed by the rather more common ECW-bodied Bristol RELL. The arrival of these buses was a clear sign that the NBC would start to impose a far more centralised control on purchasing decisions than BET had on its subsidiaries.

The early 1970s saw a number of well-established independent operators sell their business to the NBC, prompted by changes in employment laws, the death of proprietors and the belief that compulsory acquisition was imminent. On 30 April 1970 the Venture Transport Company (Newcastle) Ltd was purchased by the NBC

and placed under the control of Northern General. Venture had been established in 1938, although it could trace its roots back to 1912, and its yellow buses had been a familiar site in the Consett, Chopwell and High Spen area. Operations by Venture's own subsidiary, C & E Bus Company, passed to Northern General in September 1971. Another development of 1970 was the transfer of Wakefield's operations to Tynemouth & District, of which it had operated as a subsidiary since acquisition by Northern General in 1932.

The NBC's influence became more apparent during 1972 when the first Leyland National joined the fleet together with the arrival of both Daimler Fleetlines and Leyland Atlanteans with bodywork built by ECW. The launch of NBC's corporate identity saw poppy red replace both Northern General and Tyneside's somewhat deeper red applications and the green livery carried by Gateshead & District. Somewhat surprisingly, Sunderland District buses remained blue, receiving the relatively uncommon NBC variation of that colour. A uniform style of fleetname, with the NBC's "double N" symbol, replaced those used hitherto. Coaches began to receive all-over white with a prominent "NATIONAL" fleetname in alternating red and blue letters.

Despite the increased pressure to standardise, the innovative streak of Northern General was not quite suppressed. In 1972 two vehicles that were destined to remain unique emerged from the Bensham workshops. As already noted, the company operated a fleet of front-entrance Routemasters on some of its long-distance services. Although these vehicles were reliable and popular with both passengers and crews, they did not lend themselves to one-person operation. In a bid to address this perceived shortcoming, the company rebuilt a 1958 Leyland PD3 to normal-control layout, graced it with a Routemaster bonnet and grille and christened it the "Tynesider". It was followed by a similar rebuild of an accident-damaged Routemaster which was named the "Wearsider". Although the Tynesider saw little use in service, it did eventually find its way into preservation. The Wearsider remained in service until 1978 when it was withdrawn and sold for scrap. The conversion was not deemed a success and no further attempts were made to render the Routemaster suitable for operation by a single crew member. The Routemaster fleet therefore remained intact until 1977 when withdrawals began, although the last examples remained in service until December 1980.

Although the NBC's new image had begun to take hold on Northern General and its subsidiaries, an operating agreement with Tyneside PTE saw the introduction of a yellow livery for buses operating in the PTE, matching

Chapter 2

Go-Ahead Northern Becomes Go-Ahead Group

From local operator to national group

Go-Ahead Northern began its independent existence in an environment still in a state of flux following the upheavals of deregulation and privatisation. Competition continued to occur, necessitating frequent service changes to respond, whilst the flow of new vehicles slowed to a trickle as available funding was largely used to service the debt taken on to purchase the company.

In a move that presaged the approach that would become a common thread to the Go-Ahead story the company decided, in early 1988, to reintroduce local identities to some of its bus operations. Accordingly, on 7 February vehicles based at High Spen gained "Venture with Go-Ahead Northern" fleetnames. A similar exercise saw operations in north Tyneside adopt "The Coast Line" as a new identity whilst those in Gateshead received "Go-Ahead Northern Gateshead – In pursuit of Excellence" as a brand. Vehicles retained the company's red and white livery, although six new Renault minibuses delivered during the year received Sunderland District blue and the coach business adopted a dark red livery with "Voyager" fleetnames.

In May 1988 restructuring saw Go-Ahead Northern become a holding company for its operating subsidiaries – Northern General Transport, Northern National Omnibus and Go-Ahead Northern Engineering. In the same month the company launched the "Super Shuttle" brand for buses used on service 66, linking Gateshead Interchange with the Metro shopping centre. In June it was awarded the contract for outpatient transport in the Newcastle area, for which a fleet of London-style black taxis was purchased, whilst further expansion saw the acquisition of the long-established Newcastle firm Metro Taxis. Competition from Law Travel of Stanley between Consett and Newcastle saw the orange Leyland Nationals deployed once again.

In its early days Go-Ahead Northern faced competition on a number of its services. Several Leyland Nationals were painted orange and white during 1987 as a reserve fleet to meet such assaults. Freshly repainted 4676 (UPT 676V) is seen at Stanley depot. (Ian Athey)

on double-deck vehicles and on the cove panels of single-deck buses. Deregulation ended the integrated network operated within the Tyne & Wear PTE area and with it the yellow PTE livery carried by some buses.

It was announced that the bulk of the provisions of the 1985 Act would come into effect on 26 October 1986, quickly dubbed "D-Day". The new regime would see any operator meeting certain minimum requirements allowed to operate a service anywhere subject to registering it a minimum of 42 days prior to commencement. It also would see an end to the industry's practice of using more profitable routes to cross-subsidise the less remunerative ones. Instead, operators were required to register those services that they intended to run commercially, leaving local authorities to decide whether they should invite tenders to operate unprofitable services. The expectation was that such services would be provided by the operator submitting the lowest bid.

In the early part of the year, in order to protect the brands, the company registered the names of four of its long-dormant subsidiaries. Thus it was that the registration of the Gateshead & District Omnibus Company Ltd took effect on 26 March, followed on 9 May by that of the Tynemouth & District Omnibus Company Ltd. Five days later the Sunderland & District Omnibus Company Ltd and the Venture Transport Company Ltd completed the set.

The impact of D-Day on Northern's services was considerable and saw a significant increase in the use of minibuses, in particular. A reduction in the need for "big" buses saw most of the Leyland National 2s withdrawn, although they were held in storage as a strategic reserve in the event of a competitive attack on the company. The increasing reliance on smaller vehicles was evidenced by new bus orders for 1987, which called for 38 Alexander-bodied Renault S56 buses, each seating 19 passengers. The year also saw the final vehicles repainted out of yellow Tyne & Wear livery.

On 7 February 1987 Go-Ahead Northern Ltd was incorporated as a company, in advance of its sale by the National Bus Company.

In March 1987 a number of the stored Leyland Nationals re-entered service, carrying an all-over orange livery on a service launched in response to a competitive assault operated by Easyway Bus Services and the North East Bus Company. The vehicles did not carry fleetnames but had "Dipton Orange" branding in their windscreens. Later in the spring of 1987 the orange Nationals saw use on a service in Consett which competed against Watsons of Annfield Plain.

On 7 May 1987 it was announced that the Go-Ahead Northern management team had been successful in their bid to buy their company from the NBC, having beaten two other bidders. With 730 vehicles at the time of the sale Go-Ahead Northern was, by some margin, the largest of the NBC's bus-operating subsidiaries. For the first time in its existence it enjoyed a fully independent status rather than being a subsidiary of a larger concern.

private capital into the National Bus Company. Although thin on the detail of exactly how this would be achieved, the expectation was that such an approach would bring greater efficiency and that private enterprise would help reduce costs. In July 1984 the government's White Paper "Buses" stated that 'there is no good reason why local bus services should be provided by a national corporation' and recommended that the National Bus Company be reorganised into smaller independent units, to be sold off as private companies. Bus services would be freed from restrictions by the abolition of road service licensing except in London. It was evident, particularly given the government's large parliamentary majority, that a fundamental change to the provision of local bus services, which would impact heavily on the structure of the National Bus Company and its subsidiaries, was imminent.

The prospect of a break-up and sale of the NBC prompted relaxation of the hitherto strong controls exercised on local managers. Within Northern General an early manifestation of this was the decision to raise the company's profile by adopting a new brand – Go-Ahead Northern. One of its Bristol VRTs received a revised livery with prominent "Go-Ahead Northern – the Bus Company That Cares" branding on the 'tween-decks panels. The following year an MCW Metrobus received a rainbow livery and Go-Ahead Northern branding supplemented by the message "Don't judge a bus by its colours". Further vehicles received this livery, whilst a number of buses received liveries of the former subsidiaries and Northern General's pre-NBC scheme. Whilst this was partly driven by nostalgia, it was also clearly intended to prevent would-be competitors from capitalising on the goodwill engendered by the well-known brand names once a new competitive market emerged. Although a time of considerable uncertainty, 1985 did see new vehicles join the fleet, including the first minibuses, a batch of nine 16-seater Ford Transits which were initially used on local services in Chester-le-Street. They carried "Go-Ahead Northern MiniLink" branding. Further deliveries included Plaxton-bodied Leyland Tiger coaches, some of which were to National Express Rapide specification for use on long-distance coach services, and more Leyland Olympians with ECW bodywork. Some of these carried "Tynelink" branding for use on regional express services.

In anticipation of deregulation Northern General was reorganised on 1 September 1985 into five locally managed units, designed to make the business more responsive. The only visible sign of the change was the appearance of a strapline on vehicles containing the name of the district as an adjunct to the Go-Ahead Northern fleetname. The company also reactivated the long-dormant Northern National Omnibus Company, although the 25 vehicles transferred to it continued to carry the parent company's fleetnames.

Although many of the NBC's subsidiaries were broken up into smaller units in this period, Northern General was spared this, largely due to the fact that 70% of its operations ran under an operating agreement with Tyne & Wear PTE. This meant that it was charging Tyne & Wear fares on buses wearing Tyne & Wear livery, providing services designed by the PTE feeding the Metro. Northern had little control over commercial policy and many of its staff were subject to PTE pay and conditions. The view was that a break-up at the same time as planning for deregulation and privatisation would have overwhelmed its management resources. Furthermore, despite its fleet size, the company had a relatively compact operating area. The NBC therefore lobbied government, successfully, for it to be retained as a single entity. On the legislative front the Transport Act 1985, which included many of the provisions contained in the previous year's White Paper, received Royal Assent on 30 October 1985.

During late 1985 further livery experiments were carried out which culminated in the launch of a new brand the following February. The National Bus Company schemes were replaced with a new livery of Ayres red, relieved by white window surrounds and roof. Go-Ahead Northern fleetnames were applied below the lower-deck windows

Large numbers of Bristol VRTs joined the Northern fleet during the 1970s. Although most had bodywork by ECW, a few, including 3354 (CUP 354S) pictured in Hartlepool, were bodied by Willowbrook. (Ian Athey)

the colours, if not the exact style, of the undertaking's own vehicles. The PTE itself became Tyne & Wear following local government reorganisation in 1974 when it acquired the operations of Sunderland Corporation.

On 31 December 1974 three of Northern General's operating subsidiaries, Sunderland District, Tynemouth & District and Venture, ceased to exist, with all services and vehicles passing to the parent company. Twelve months later the remaining subsidiaries, Gateshead & District and Tyneside Omnibus Co ceased trading. New vehicle deliveries throughout the latter part of the 1970s were very much NBC standard fare – Leyland Nationals, ECW-bodied Bristol VRTs and Park Royal-bodied Leyland Atlanteans, whilst coaching needs were largely met by Plaxton-bodied Leyland Leopards. Some variety was provided in 1978/9 by a number of Bristol VRTs with Willowbrook bodywork. Many of the company's deliveries in the early 1970s had been built with dual doors, as these were considered at the time to help speed up the boarding process on one-person-operated services. Subsequent experience showed, however, that in addition to introducing an avoidable risk in terms of passenger injury, the existence of a central exit could cause structural problems. As a result a programme of removing the second doorway was initiated.

On 11 August 1980 the first stage of the Tyne & Wear Metro opened from Haymarket, in the centre of Newcastle, to Tynemouth, with the second phase, linking Heworth and Gateshead to Newcastle city centre, opening on 22 November. The PTE's plans for the new network were based upon integration of transport and encouraging passengers to travel by Metro wherever practicable. This meant curtailing many long-standing bus services at either Gateshead or Heworth where new interchanges were built. Although admirable in principle, it is now recognised that forcing passengers to change modes was not universally acclaimed by those customers who had to experience the reality. The integrationist aspirations of the PTE also saw the yellow-based livery carried by Northern General's buses (as well as those of fellow NBC subsidiary United) modified to replicate the exact style of the PTE's own buses. Tyne & Wear Transport fleetnames, augmented by the NBC logo, appeared on the sides of buses with the operator's name relegated to the front dash panel.

Fleet developments during the period saw the last Leyland Atlanteans, this time with Roe bodies, arrive during 1980, together with the first Leyland National 2s, an upgraded model that eliminated many of the weaknesses of earlier vehicles. A batch of MCW Metrobuses also joined the fleet, making Northern General one of only three NBC subsidiaries to receive the type, together with the first Leyland Olympians, launched as a replacement for the Bristol VRT.

The reduction in new bus intake during 1981 anticipated lean times ahead, as a deteriorating economic climate combined with the abolition of the new bus grant forced operators to scale back on investment plans. That said, 1983 saw small numbers of new Leylands – both Nationals and Olympians – delivered, together with a brace of Leyland's new Royal Tiger Doyen coach. Two similar vehicles joined the fleet in 1984, together with five Plaxton-bodied Leyland Leopard coaches.

The Conservative Party's 1983 election manifesto contained a commitment to relax bus licensing, encourage the creation of smaller units in place of the monolithic public transport organisations and introduce substantial

Although early deliveries to the newly privatised Go-Ahead Northern were minibuses, a number of full-size vehicles did join the fleet. One of five Alexander-bodied Leyland Olympians to join the fleet during 1989, 3679 (G679 TCN) heads into Newcastle, hotly pursued by an ECW-bodied Leyland Leopard carrying Expresslink livery. (Ian Athey)

During 1989 the company received new full-size vehicles - Leyland Lynx and DAF/Optare single-deck buses and Alexander-bodied Leyland Olympian double-deckers. Two Plaxton-bodied coaches, for use on National Express Rapide services, and a number of Iveco minibuses also arrived. In addition, there was a large influx of second-hand vehicles, mainly Ford Transit minibuses destined for the Metro Taxis fleet, whilst a programme to refurbish and re-engine some of the Leyland National 2 fleet was initiated.

In January 1989 Derby City Council indicated that it wished to sell Derby City Transport, its bus operating company. Although Go-Ahead Northern was unsuccessful, it provided an indication of the type of business that would feature in future expansion plans. The company also showed that it would seek growth by local acquisition when, in May, it acquired the Gypsy Queen operations of the Langley Park Motor Company, which continued as a separate subsidiary. Later in the year Stanley-based Law Travel, with which it had been competing, was also acquired, although on this occasion the vehicles were disposed of quickly. An interesting acquisition in November was that of the Tyne & Wear Omnibus Company, which was competing heavily with Busways, the former bus operations of Tyne & Wear PTE. This operation was acquired by Coolfirm Ltd, a subsidiary established earlier in the year by Go-Ahead Northern, and sold on the same day to Busways.

The most unusual acquisition, though, was that of twenty public houses sold by Scottish & Newcastle Breweries as part of its estates disposal required to comply with a Monopolies and Mergers Commission report into the brewing industry. A new subsidiary, Go-Ahead Leisure Ltd, was established to manage this part of the business. Although profitable, the business was a non-core activity and it was sold to the Second Pub Estate Company for £3.2m on 16 February 1996.

The early 1990s were to prove a challenging time for the company as falling passenger numbers, caused by population decline, job losses, growing car ownership and the Metro system, required economies to be made. Metro Taxis was successful in retaining its health-authority contract but it was smaller in scope than that held previously. Although only five new buses joined the fleet, a large number of vehicles were withdrawn as retrenchment began to take its toll.

Another area in which economies were sought was that of staff costs. In addition to requiring fewer staff to serve what was now a smaller operation, the company also had to address the differential pay and conditions of service at those garages within the former Tyne & Wear PTE area. This meant that some drivers were earning around

The vehicle evaluation trials of 1989 saw a number of Leyland Lynx and DAF/Optare Deltas join the fleet. One of the latter, 4738 (G738 RTY), is seen in Durham when new. Further similar vehicles joined the fleet in subsequent years and a small number were acquired with the operations of OK Travel. (Author's collection)

The early 1990s saw Go-Ahead Northern establish a number of operating subsidiaries. In 1992 the Tyneside Omnibus Co subsidiary rebranded its services as VFM Buses. The two-tone blue livery adopted for this operation is seen here on 8009 (J609 KCU), one of 89 Wright Handybus-bodied Dennis Darts that joined the fleet between 1991 and 1993. (A. D. Glen)

one-third more than those in County Durham. Although some staff accepted an offer to buy out their legacy terms with a lump-sum payment, there remained a number of unresolved issues as the company sought to devolve pay bargaining to garage level. In April 1991 workers at Chester-le-Street, Consett and Stanley took strike action, ostensibly over a pay claim, which quickly spread to other locations. After nearly a month the dispute was referred to arbitration and an improved offer recommended, which allowed for a return to work. Several other operators had provided services during the strike and some of these continued running after the dispute ended, further exacerbating pressure on the company.

From the beginning of 1991 a new structure was adopted which saw the creation of five operating subsidiaries, each with significant autonomy to meet local challenges. These were:

Northern General Transport Co, trading as Go-Ahead Northern, operating out of Chester-le-Street, Consett and Stanley;
Gateshead & District Omnibus Co, trading as Go-Ahead Gateshead, operating from Gateshead and Winlaton;
Tyneside Omnibus Company, trading as South Tyne Buses, from South Shields;
Tynemouth & District Omnibus Company, trading as Coastline Buses, from Percy Main and Wallsend; and
Sunderland & District Omnibus Company, trading as Wear Buses from Sunderland, Washington and Philadelphia.
The Metro Taxis, Gypsy Queen and Voyager businesses continued unchanged.

Despite the upheavals caused by industrial action and restructuring, the company demonstrated confidence in the future by resuming fleet renewal during 1991. The first of 89 Wright Handybus-bodied Dennis Darts arrived during the autumn and were joined by 14 Optare MetroRider minibuses which received MetroCentre Minis livery. The newly established operating subsidiaries also expressed their commercial and operational freedom by

Operations in Gateshead were rebranded as Go-Ahead Gateshead and vehicles were painted in a striking red, white and blue scheme in which Metrobus 2771 (C771 OCN) has been preserved. (Steven Hodgson)

The reactivated Sunderland & District subsidiary adopted a two-tone green livery and "Wear Buses" fleetname as shown by 2767 (C767 OCN). (Author's collection)

introducing new liveries. Go-Ahead Gateshead adopted a red and white livery with a bold blue skirt and upward stripe, whilst the Coastline operations of Tyneside employed a traditional red-and-cream application and Wear Buses opted for two-tone green. The Northern brand was also refreshed and relaunched, with buses carrying a "proud of our routes" strapline on their red and white livery. In January 1992 the South Shields operations of Tyneside adopted a new two-tone blue scheme and the fleetname VFM, signifying value for money. The relaunch of brands was generally accompanied by a package of customer service undertakings designed to win back passenger confidence.

In early 1992, following an announcement that the Metro was to be extended to Sunderland, Go-Ahead Northern revealed plans for a Guided Transport Expressway (GTE) which it argued would be both cheaper and more flexible than a rail-based system. Despite the potentially significant cost savings Tyne & Wear PTE proceeded with the Metro option and GTE was quietly shelved.

Further expansion took place in June with the acquisition of Robert Tindall Coaches (Tyneside) Ltd, based in Low Fell. Operating as Low Fell Coaches, the business was most notable for the way it had, against strong objections from Tyne & Wear PTE, obtained a licence to operate a cross-Tyne service linking Low Fell with Newcastle in 1983, when most services terminated at local Metro stations. The operation, with its blue and white livery, remained as a separate subsidiary. Shortly afterwards it was the turn of Shaw's Coaches of Craghead to join the growing Go-Ahead Northern fleet. Operated using the Venture licence, Shaw's retained its own identity.

During the spring of 1993 the company had to contend with significant competition from both Classic Coaches of Annfield Plain and Gardiners of Spennymoor on services between Chester-le-Street, Stanley and Newcastle. It responded by increasing its own services which were operated by Shaw's.

In November 1993 Go-Ahead Northern made its first acquisition outside the company's north-east heartland when it purchased Brighton & Hove Bus and Coach Company. This part of the story, and that of the other operations since acquired, are described separately. In a clear statement of intent that the company saw scope

Northern General, with operations based at Consett, Stanley and Chester-le-Street, adopted a red and white livery with "Northern – proud of our roots" fleetname. Metrobus 3505 (UTN 505Y) demonstrates. (Steven Hodgson)

Go-Ahead Northern acquired the long-established Metro Taxis business in 1988. Although much of its work was contract hire, it also operated a number of local services, largely using minibuses. A small number of double-deck buses were operated, however, including 3554 (MBR 454T), an ECW-bodied Leyland Atlantean seen in Byker during September 1995. (John Young)

for future growth outside the north-east, its name was changed to The Go-Ahead Group plc with effect from 1 February 1994. This was followed by a stock market flotation which raised over £12 million and valued the Group at about £40 million. Trading in its shares on the London Stock Exchange started on 9 May 1994.

In early 1994 the long-established operator OK Travel of Bishop Auckland initiated a number of competitive services in the Newcastle, Gateshead and Sunderland areas. In response, a new outstation was established in OK's home town to operate a number of local services, and frequencies were boosted on other routes. By August the bus war, which had attracted adverse local press coverage, was over, with both sides cancelling registrations for the new competitive services and returning to their previous pattern. Further competition was experienced in the Gateshead area from Classic Buses, which prompted the launch of a new brand, Tyne Rider, using a fleet of green MCW Metrobuses. In July 1994 the Group submitted a bid for council-owned Darlington Transport, although the sale did not occur as the operation went into administration before completion following Stagecoach's decision to register competitive services over its entire network. A further Go-Ahead acquisition during the year saw the six-vehicle business of Hammel's of Stanley placed under control of Venture although retaining the previous owner's livery and Diamond fleetname.

In 1995 the Coastline operation received five of the first low-floor buses for use in the United Kingdom. The vehicles, Wright Pathfinder-bodied Dennis Lance SLFs, were used on services 325 and 326, which linked the Metro at North Shields with Whitley Bay and the North Tyneside Hospital. The local authority supported the initiative by providing suitable roadside infrastructure. Other new arrivals during the year included 14 Optare Sigma-bodied Dennis Lances for Gateshead, further MetroRiders and more Dennis Darts with both Marshall and Plaxton bodywork. In addition, and reflecting the Group's new status as a national operator, 120 Marshall-bodied Darts were ordered for delivery between 1995 and 1997, although only 80 of these would be destined for fleets in the north-east.

A significant acquisition during 1995 was the long-established OK Motor Services of Bishop Auckland. Full integration of the business was delayed by a Monopolies and Mergers Commission report. Seen in OK livery, but with Go-Ahead Northern fleetnames, is Alexander-bodied Leyland Atlantean 3793 (AVK 152V). This bus was new to Tyne & Wear PTE. (Steven Hodgson)

In 1995 Coastline was one of the first in the UK to place low-floor buses into service. Five Wright Pathfinder-bodied Dennis Lances, including 4772 (M422 FJR), were introduced onto services 325 and 326 in Whitley Bay. (Chris Redpath)

On 22 March 1995 Go-Ahead acquired OK Travel for £5.35 million. It had been clear for some time, following the death of the owner, Wade Emmerson, son of the founder, that the remaining members of the family would seek to sell the long-established business. The purchase attracted an investigation from the Office of Fair Trading because of its potential effect on competition in the area and, pending its completion, Go-Ahead was unable to take any steps to integrate services with its existing operations. The OFT delivered its verdict in February 1996 when it reported that not only was OK Travel in a poor financial state but that there would continue to be sufficient competition from other operators in the region. In giving evidence the Group explained that OK Travel would continue to enjoy a separate existence as its low-cost subsidiary. Approval of the acquisition led to withdrawal of those services where OK Travel had been competing with Go-Ahead's existing services followed by transfer of some operations to other subsidiaries to align operating bases and routes more intelligently.

June 1995 saw the purchase of Armstrongs Coaches of Ebchester, with the fleet operated as part of the OK Travel subsidiary. The year saw further new vehicles joining the Group, including a small batch of Plaxton Verde-bodied Volvo B10Bs, part of a larger group order, joining the Gateshead fleet. The acquisition of OK Travel served as the catalyst for a fundamental review of operations. This led to a reorganisation within the Group which saw the creation of a dedicated post of Managing Director North East, a rôle taken by Paul Matthews, with overall responsibility for all bus operations within the region. These developments reflected the fact that the Group's management efforts were now largely focused on overseeing its growing national portfolio, and provided a single leadership focus for the north-east operations. There was also a rationalisation of operating licences, with those held by Low Fell and Gypsy Queen transferring to OK along with the Voyager coach operations, whilst the Venture licence was passed to Northern General.

During the latter half of the 1990s low-floor single-deck buses became the norm and, from 1997 when a batch of Optare's distinctively-styled Excel was received, all future deliveries were to this layout. Further Optare products arrived the following year when the first Solos began to displace older step-entrance minibuses from the fleet. Further investment in fleet renewal saw large numbers of Wright-bodied single-deckers arrive on Volvo and Scania chassis together with a small number of Wrightbus's Cadet, based upon DAF (and later VDL) running units. In addition large numbers of the popular and versatile Plaxton Pointer-bodied Dennis Dart, subsequently marketed as a Transbus and then an ADL product, have been delivered.

Chapter 3

Go North East
Proud of its roots

In May 1998 the OK Travel coaching business was sold to Classic of Annfield Plain, followed a month later by the formal transfer of OK's services operating from Bishop Auckland to Go Northern, with those at Peterlee, where the depot closed, passing to Go Wear which operated services from Philadelphia. The sale of the coaching operations meant that coaching activity was restricted to National Express contracts.

The opportunity was taken to reorganise the business, with four operating companies, Go-Northern, Go-Gateshead, Go-Coastline and Go-Wear adopting a common livery of red and blue with a standard fleetname style. This approach ensured that the right balance was struck between creating a single, trusted brand and retaining the benefits of localised management and accountability.

The election of a Labour government in 1997 brought a changed emphasis in delivery of local transport with an increased focus on integration and high quality. Increasingly, local authorities began to recognise the value of working in partnership with bus operators, ensuring that investment in infrastructure improvements and bus priority measures was met by the provision of high-quality vehicles. A good example of this approach was the launch of the Durham Road "Super Route" in Sunderland during 1998. The year also saw the company take only its second batch of new double-deckers since privatisation when 23 Volvo Olympians with Northern Counties Palatine II bodywork joined the fleet. They were initially allocated to South Shields where they replaced a number of NBC-era double-deckers.

In 1997 the operations in the region were reorganised as Go North East with four trading divisions and striking new livery was adopted. The Go-Xpress brand was adopted for certain long-distance services, as seen on 3851, a DAF/Optare Spectra transferred from London Central. (Richard Godfrey)

Four Wright-bodied Scania articulated buses were introduced onto service X66, linking the Metro Centre with Gateshead. They carried a simplified livery that was adopted, in modified form, for the rest of the fleet together with the Go North East fleetname.

In 1999 a new depot was opened in Deptford, Sunderland, which replaced outdated facilities at Philadelphia and Park Lane Sunderland, allowing the latter to be redeveloped as a new interchange.

Go North East played a key role in developing Traveline North East, the integrated public-transport information service which went live in February 2000, ahead of much of the rest of the country. Fleet developments during the year saw the first low-floor double-deck buses, East Lancs-bodied Dennis Tridents, delivered. Other double-deck arrivals were a number of Optare Spectra double-deckers transferred from London Central where they had been displaced by contract changes.

Four Wright Solar Fusion-bodied Scanias, the first articulated buses for a Go-Ahead Group company, entered service during 2001 on the Metrocentre Express service X66. Their silver-based livery was applied in a simpler style than that used hitherto and, anticipating a decision to adopt the Go North East brand across the fleets, they carried Go North East fleetnames rather than the local brand name. The application of local fleetnames above the driver's cab continued for a short while before these too were phased out. The articulated buses were provided in connection with the launch of the Centrelink Partnership, which saw a total of £21 million invested by Nexus (as Tyne & Wear PTE had become), Go North East and Capital Shopping Centres, owners of the Metro Centre. It delivered a rebuilt bus station at the centre and a buses-only access bridge across the railway line, which helped improve service reliability.

In March 2002 the Tyne & Wear Metro was extended to Sunderland. Although travel patterns had changed during its construction, its opening still impacted on passenger numbers as users transferred to the subsidised service. The cost of supporting Metro services also forced Nexus to make cuts in its budgets elsewhere, most notably to its concessionary travel scheme, which had a further impact on the numbers of passengers using local bus services.

Since privatisation Go North East had focused its fleet renewal on single-deck buses, including significant numbers of mini- and midibuses which had taken on a greater importance than hitherto. By 2004, however, the remaining double-deckers from NBC days were in need of replacement. The company was able to take 45 six-year old Volvo Olympians, displaced prematurely from London fleets by the introduction of low-floor buses. Prior to entering service they benefited from an extensive refurbishment, including conversion to single doorway.

September 2004 saw the opening of the Silverlink Guided Busway and the launch of route 19, linking the Cobalt Business Park with both the Metro and the Shields Ferry, the last remaining cross-Tyne ferry service. Nexus funded a

In 2005 Go North East gained a number of schools contracts for which a fleet of Leyland and Volvo Olympians was acquired. Still carrying its previous owners' livery, 3947 (H481 PVW) is seen in Sunderland. The bus was new to Dublin Bus but subsequently passed to Isle of Man Transport. (Steven Hodgson)

To help speed up the introduction of low-floor buses, a number of second-hand vehicles were acquired during 2005. 8287 (V437 KGF) was new to Limebourne.

number of infrastructure improvements, including a new ferry stage and Metro station with a park-and-ride facility at Northumberland Park, whilst Go Coastline provided a high-frequency service using six new Wright-bodied Scania single-deckers in a distinctive livery, fitted with guide wheels to allow their use on the guided sections of road.

Additions to the fleet in 2004 included 24 Marshall-bodied Dennis Darts transferred from Go-Ahead London to replace the Optare Excels which had proved to be unreliable and expensive to maintain. Together with further second-hand acquisitions, these helped to remove a number of older, step-entrance buses from the fleet. A notable milestone during the year was the withdrawal from passenger service of the last Leyland Nationals within the Go-Ahead Group, marking the end of an association with the type that started in May 1972 when the first examples were delivered to Northern General. The last few examples survived for another two years as driver trainers.

In January 2005 further streamlining of operations saw the end of the Go Coastline operation, with South Shields depot closing and Percy Main transferring to the Gateshead fleet. The decision to scale back on operations had been taken partly as a result of significant losses of passengers caused by the opening of the Metro to Sunderland.

Fleet additions during the year included three Wright Eclipse Gemini-bodied Volvo B7TL double-deckers in a distinctive livery, applied with the use of printed vinyls, for the X10 service linking Newcastle and Middlesbrough. These vehicles brought new standards of comfort, with radio programmes available together with an "in flight" magazine and specially designed seat coverings with a pattern featuring local landmarks. A dedicated driver roster was also developed for the service. In addition, the capture of a number of schools contracts from the start of the 2005/06 academic year saw an eclectic range of double-deckers join the fleet, including examples of Leyland Olympians from both Dublin Bus and Isle of Man Transport. A number of similar vehicles also arrived on loan from Ensignbus, although all had left the fleet by the end of the year.

The year also saw the relaunch of the 93/94 Loop in Gateshead, funded in part by a grant from the government's Kickstart initiative, designed to help develop bus use as an alternative to the car; it saw the doubling of frequency of

In 2005 three Wright-bodied Volvo B7TLs entered service on route X10, linking Newcastle with Middlesbrough. They carried a dedicated livery which was the beginning of a new approach to marketing services. 3943 (NK05 GZR) is seen arriving in Newcastle.

The former OK Motor Services depot in Bishop Auckland closed in April 2006. Two Leyland Olympians, acquired with the business, are seen "on shed" shortly before closure. (Gary Mitchelhill)

an orbital route connecting Gateshead's major hospital with a wide area of the town and the introduction of low-floor buses. The route was a good example of those targeted by the scheme, which focused on providing pump-priming funding to service enhancements that would otherwise have been viewed as marginal from a commercial perspective.

In October 2005 a revised livery was launched, of a similar style to that used by buses on the X10 service but utilising the standard fleet colours of red, blue and yellow. Amongst the first vehicles to carry the scheme were six DAF SB220GS/Plaxton Prestige single-deckers previously used on airport services by Speedlink.

In April 2006 the former OK depot in Bishop Auckland closed, most local services and a number of vehicles passing to Arriva, which operated them from its existing premises in the town; this move effectively marked the end of the OK story. Go North East still maintained a local presence and introduced four new Wright-bodied Volvo double-deckers on service 724, linking the town with Newcastle.

A major review of the Go North East business, undertaken in 2005 by Peter Huntley of transport consultancy TAS Partnership, identified the need for a significant change in strategy, in order to address falling passenger numbers and, hence, profitability. Peter was appointed Managing Director in 2006 to implement a new business plan, the most obvious implications of which were demonstrated in the fleet, network and branding policies. Behind the scenes an internal restructure and raising of driver pay rates was undertaken to address staffing and reliability problems.

Market research had established that there was a poor association with the Go North East fleet name. This, combined with the fact that Go North East was generally not the network operator in the region, prompted the decision to manage individual service groups as brands. A comprehensive review resulted in the establishment of a three-tier (Grade A, B and C) structure with a strong emphasis on the development of "turn up and go" high-frequency operations. Although initially controversial, the radical simplification of the network, in conjunction with branding and vehicle initiatives, has succeeded in reversing passenger loss, and profitability has increased markedly.

Each brand effectively operates as a small bus company under the Go North East umbrella, with its own vehicles, staff, service manager, cost and revenue budgets and targets. Over 50 brands have been introduced with a strong emphasis on identities proposed by staff and customers. These include Red Kites, Angel, Cobalt Clipper, Prince Bishops, MetroLink and Drifter with strong local associations, "aspirational" brands such as Red Arrows, Orbit, Ten, CityLink, Laser and Tyne-Tees Express, unique Geordie "cultural" identities such as Lambton Worm and recognition of respected former operators such as Venture. The new approach acknowledges that the most profitable services

In September 2006 Arriva North East began competing with Go North East's established services between Gateshead and Saltwell Park. Dennis Dart 8171 (S371 ONL), seen in front of the competition at Gateshead Interchange, shows a modified livery style based on that used by buses on service X10. (Steven Hodgson)

In 2006 Go North East implemented a new business plan which saw the network revised with key routes operated as sub-businesses in their own right with a distinctive livery. The highest-profile routes gained new vehicles such as Scania OmniCity 5255 (NK56 KJE) which carries branding for the Cobalt Clipper.

justify the newest buses whilst mid-life vehicles are used on lower-profile but still commercially worthwhile routes. Buses used on branded routes carry a single-colour base livery with vinyls being used to display the branding itself. By using the same base colour for more than one corridor, only a change of vinyl is required when vehicles are transferred.

The fleet structure was changed, with midibus purchase ended and small-vehicle needs concentrated on a single vehicle type, the Mini Pointer Dart. New heavy-duty single-deckers, Mercedes-Benz Citaro and Scania OmniCitys with high-specification interiors and air-conditioning, were delivered for Grade A routes whilst a major programme of refurbishment was launched for Grade B services, which saw mid-life Scania and Volvo single-deck vehicles returned to "as new" condition from the passenger perspective.

Although Go North East had experienced significant levels of competition since deregulation, this had largely come from smaller independent operators rather than other companies within the so-called "big groups". During the summer of 2006 Stagecoach, which had acquired the Busways business in July 1994, introduced a service which followed the same route as the recently relaunched "Magic Roundabout" service 42 in Sunderland.

In September 2006 Arriva's North East subsidiary started operating a service linking Gateshead with Saltwell Park, a route covered by Go North East's routes 53 and 54, although they were deregistered before even commencing operations. The service ceased from November. Arriva's move was no doubt prompted by Go North East's decision to launch a number of services over routes operated by Arriva. These included a half-hourly service linking Hartlepool and

Each route brand is supported by dedicated publicity.

"Yellow Bus" branding is applied to buses used on contract services although, as seen here, vehicles from this fleet do see use on scheduled services. Northern Counties-bodied Volvo Olympian 3916 (R274 LGH) is one of a number of similar vehicles acquired from Go-Ahead's London fleets. (Steven Hodgson)

Sunderland, and a Durham local service rather cornily branded the "Pink Panther". The latter service did not last beyond the end of the year, however. Of a more enduring nature was the service introduced between Newcastle and Blyth which saw the yellow Olympians gain "Bargain-Bus" branding to provide an unashamedly low-cost alternative to Arriva's more established offering on this corridor. Arriva responded by launching an express service linking Durham with Newcastle.

During the spring of 2007 an experimental park-and-ride service was introduced, linking the Metro Centre and Newcastle city centre. Although the service was withdrawn after 18 months, it did nevertheless represent a significant development in the region, as Nexus had previously channelled all park-and-ride traffic onto its own Metro services rather than using buses. The service used Optare Solos in a dedicated livery.

A number of local independent operators offered their bus operations to Go North East in 2007. In March the local bus services and premises of Ashington-based Northumbria Coaches were acquired, which brought with it a number of Leyland Lynx and Tiger vehicles together with a unique Plaxton Concept 2000-bodied Volvo B6BLE. The acquisition allowed for the Bargain Bus fleet, together with a number of schools workings, to be reallocated from the overcrowded Percy Main depot. The operation was rebranded "Northumbria Buses" in order to draw a clear distinction with the coach operation, which was not acquired. Further operations sold to Go North East included Peterlee-based Jayline on 4 June 2007, whilst in October the bus operations of Stanley Taxis, together with 14 vehicles, were taken over. The Stanley business gained the Venture brand adopted for services in Consett.

The acquisition of smaller companies continued into 2008 and on 28 January the commercial bus operations and associated assets of Sunderland-based Redby Buses were acquired. The month also saw the launch of the East Gateshead Quality Partnership, which brought the company together with Nexus and Gateshead Council. It saw the launch of three new brands: the Loop, the Crusader and Team Valley Clipper. Key aspects of the arrangement included a pledge by Go North East to maintain timetables for at least 12 months, not to increase fares unless operating costs increased and an undertaking to operate only low-floor buses. Nexus provided high standards of passenger information at stops and ensured that shelters were properly maintained, whilst the council implemented schemes to tackle traffic congestion. A notable feature was the establishment of a board, with representation from all three partners, to monitor progress and ensure any problems were swiftly addressed.

An innovative approach to green transport was initiated in the summer of 2009 when Go North East became the first UK bus operator to allow passengers to take unfolded bicycles on its vehicles. Initially launched on a six-month trial basis, nine Wright-bodied Volvo B10BLE buses were deployed on the service, branded "Lime", which links Consett and Sunderland and runs parallel with the eastern end of the Workington to Sunderland coast-to-coast cycle path. A fee of £2 is charged for cycles which are accommodated in the wheelchair bay of the bus. The area used for bikes is shared with passengers using a wheelchair or with children in buggies, so if someone using a wheelchair wants to travel when a bike is already on board, the driver will ask the cyclist to give up their space. Cyclists are under no obligation to leave the bus, however, if they do, they are entitled to a full single fare refund plus £2. The company's market research indicated that such a conflict was unlikely to occur as demand for cycle space tends to occur at the beginning and end of the day, whilst buggy and wheelchair demand is usually greatest between 09:00 and 16:00.

In July 2009 the first of Optare's integral Versa buses delivered to a Go-Ahead subsidiary entered service on the Saltwell Park routes, quickly followed by similar vehicles for the "Drifter" service in Sunderland. This type

In March 2007 Go North East acquired the bus operations of Northumbria Coaches. The fleet included the unique Plaxton Concept-bodied Volvo B6, NK54 PHV, caught on camera heading along Sandyford Road in Jesmond followed by an Arriva Enviro400. (Gary Mitchelhill)

has been selected to replace the ageing midibus fleet as it provides both greater capacity and a better customer environment than the vehicles used previously.

Although Arriva North East and Go North East had been competing heavily for a number of years, it was announced in October 2009 that both operators had negotiated a deal which would see Arriva take on the Ashington operations of Go North East whilst Go North East would assume Arriva's Hexham operations. The transfer was conditional on receiving approval from the Office of Fair Trading, which was granted in February 2010. The exchange of routes took place on 29 March and the attendant service changes marked an end to the Bargain Bus operation between Blyth and Newcastle.

A comprehensive recasting of services linking Newcastle, the Metro Centre and Hexham was undertaken and in August the first phase of the new timetable was launched, which took into account the views of customers using services through the Tyne Valley. The improved timetable provided three buses an hour between Hexham and Newcastle, whilst new Mercedes-Benz Citaro buses carrying "ten" branding represented a fresh start compared to the vehicles previously used. From November the second phase of the rebranding saw the introduction of two new brands, "Tynedale Links" and the "Toon Link", to accompany the launch of improved local services in the area.

From the beginning of 2010 a further streamlining of Go North East's structures took place when the Go Wear operating licence was surrendered. Henceforth there would be two companies operating under the Go North East banner – Go Northern Ltd, the South division, which operated from Deptford, Washington, Stanley and Chester-le-Street depots, and Go North East Ltd, the North division, with services running from Gateshead, Percy Main, Winlaton and Hexham. Vehicles from both companies carry Go North East fleetnames and there are frequent transfers between the two companies.

In common with a number of operators, the advent of free nationwide bus travel for pensioners in April 2008 had a significant impact on the demand for services. A particular consequence of this has been that smaller vehicles now have less of a role in the Go North East fleet than in previous years, as it has been more cost-effective to meet growing demand by using larger buses than increasing frequencies. This change meant that by early 2010 the Optare Solo fleet had all been withdrawn, although several vehicles were transferred to the Go South Coast and Plymouth Citybus fleets where they replaced older minibuses. Other fleet developments during the year saw a number of buses transfer from other Go-Ahead Group companies. These included Volvo B10BLEs with Wright

Between 2006 and 2010 Go North East competed heavily with Arriva North East on routes linking Blyth and Newcastle. Carrying yellow livery and "Bargain Bus" branding, 4875 (N950 TVK), an Alexander Strider-bodied Volvo B10B acquired with the business of Redby in 2002, heads away from Whitley Bay.

In March 2010 Go North East and Arriva North Eas`t effected a depot swap which saw Go North East acquire services operating from Hexham whilst its Ashington depot passed to Arriva. Amongst the vehicles acquired was 5146 (V532 GDS), a Wright-bodied Volvo B10 seen in Newcastle. A comprehensive recast of services linking Hexham and Newcastle/Gateshead took place in the summer of 2010. (Steven Hodgson)

bodywork from Oxford and a batch of Volvo Olympians from Metrobus, which carry the "Yellow Bus" brand adopted in 2007 for schools, work and other local authority contracts.

In the summer of 2010 Go North East was successful in winning the Nexus contract to operate Quaylink, a two-route service linking major bus, Metro and rail stations with waterfront attractions such as The Sage at Gateshead. A brand-new fleet of environmentally friendly Optare Versa buses, built to the latest Euro 5 EEV emissions standards and carrying a distinctive bright yellow livery, was introduced. The vehicles also carry names of famous local residents.

Completion of the bulk of the network restructure by 2010 permitted attention to be given to a major rationalisation of fares and ticketing with greatly simplified scales, zonal and flat-fare arrangements in each urban area and new initiatives on fares discounts through the BuzzFare and Cheap Day Return initiatives. The company is also leading a regional effort to establish a multi-operator, multi-modal smartcard system, with its own smartcard system in operation by early 2011 and a common platform with Metro and other bus operators to ensure maximum impact and inter-operability.

By the beginning of 2011 Go North East's five-year programme to overhaul its network had been completed and the image of the company had changed fundamentally with over 50% of customers using a network of high-frequency "turn up and go" services operated by modern low-floor buses with distinctive brands. The change had been implemented in a gradual way in order to avoid changing long-established networks too radically in one stage, although inevitably some traditional routes had been lost. During the summer of 2011 Go North East began operating a number of services previously provided by Veolia, on behalf of Nexus. A fleet of Optare Solo buses carrying Nexus Bus red and grey livery and "Buses" fleetname was acquired for these services. In addition, two similar vehicles with hybrid diesel-electric drive helped launch Sunderland Connect, a new service.

Peter Huntley stepped down as Managing Director in December 2011 to focus on other activities, primarily a trek to the North Pole to raise funds for Transaid, a charity that aims to reduce poverty and improve livelihoods across Africa and the developing world through creating better transport. Sadly, his plans did not come to fruition. On 19 February 2012, whilst training for the trip in the Lake District, he was killed in a climbing accident. Peter's successor as MD is Kevin Carr, who joined Northern General in 1975 as an apprentice electrician since when he has worked in a variety of roles within the Go North East business.

Passenger growth on some services has now reached a level where extra capacity is required. To meet this need further double-deck buses, both new and examples cascaded from London, have joined the fleet, together with articulated buses surplus to Go-Ahead London's requirements as a result of the decision to withdraw these vehicles from service in the capital. During 2012 "the Angel" service, linking Newcastle and Durham, will receive 15 Volvo B5LH hybrid buses, part-funded by the government's Green Bus Grant.

Despite the increase in passenger numbers and high passenger satisfaction levels achieved by Go North East, the Tyne & Wear Integrated Transport Authority (ITA) and Nexus, its passenger transport executive, are seeking to introduce a franchising approach to local bus services within the region. Go North East believes that this will increase costs and reduce passenger choice and has launched its Charter for Positive Change to fight these proposals.

The company has not lost touch with its roots and has adopted a new red livery, with a revived "Northern" identity, for those services that do not have route-branded vehicles and to replace the rather bland white livery used previously for engineering spares. In addition, in early 2012 it reintroduced local services in Bishop Auckland, resurrecting the OK Motor Services brand in what would have been that operator's centenary.

As Go-Ahead reaches its silver jubilee, the North East business from which it grew, and which reaches its own centenary in 2013, is clearly in good shape to face the future.

Go North East was awarded the contract to operate Newcastle/Gateshead's high-profile Quaylink service from July 2010, for which nine Optare Versas were ordered, joining similar vehicles delivered the previous year. 8310 (NK10 GNY) is seen at The Sage, Gateshead.

The success of Go North East's revised route network has led to a dramatic increase in passenger numbers. As a result higher-capacity vehicles are now required for some services. In April 2011 six new Wright Gemini 2-bodied Volvo B9TLs helped provide a welcome boost to Red Arrow X1 between Newcastle and Easington Lane. 6003 (NK11 BHD) is seen at Gateshead Interchange.

For those services that are not route branded Go North East has adopted a red livery with "Northern" fleetnames. Having just crossed the Tyne by way of the High Level Bridge, 3878 (W188SCU) is caught on camera entering Gateshead.

The year 2012 would have been the centenary of OK Motor Services and so it is appropriate that the OK brand was resurrected by Go North East for services in and around Bishop Auckland. Go North East 5229 (NK55 OLG) is seen in Bishop Auckland on 27 March 2012.

Chapter 4

Brighton & Hove
Essential travel for the city

The current Brighton & Hove Bus and Coach Company has its roots in the Brighton, Hove & Preston United Omnibus Company, established in 1884. When Brighton Corporation introduced tram services in 1901, the company, although not competing with the Corporation trams directly, decided to begin replacing the horse buses with motor buses. In 1911 it obtained powers to operate trolleybuses, although these were purchased by Brighton Corporation in 1913.

In 1916 Thomas Tilling, an established bus operator in London at the time, acquired Brighton, Hove & Preston United, replaced the remaining horse buses with motor buses and embarked upon a programme of expansion. Tilling had been extending its operations throughout the country, and whilst it generally adopted local identities for its bus interests outside London, those in Brighton and Hove were operated under its own name.

In the mid-1930s the urban area of Brighton was expanding, driven by the ease of commuting into London on the newly electrified Southern Railway. Brighton Corporation, by repute the largest English town without its own municipal buses, was keen to extend services beyond the limits of the tram network and commissioned a report which advocated purchase of Tilling's operations within the borough and reaching a suitable accommodation with Southdown. It is not clear whether this proposal forced Tilling to establish the local credentials of its Sussex operation but on 26 November 1935 the Brighton, Hove & District Omnibus Company (BH&D) was incorporated as a wholly-owned subsidiary of Thomas Tilling Ltd to operate services in the area.

In July 1937, Brighton Council and BH&D reached an agreement on co-ordination, providing for the pooling of receipts and running expenses in the ratio of 72½% to the company and 27½% to the Corporation. The agreement was confirmed by the Brighton Corporation (Transport) Act the following year. A joint operating area came into force on 1 April 1939 covering Brighton, Hove, Portslade, Rottingdean and Southwick, although Southdown Motor Services routes within the borough were not included. Both fleets adopted a common Tilling red and cream livery with "Brighton, Hove & District" fleetnames. Vehicles operated by the Corporation also carried Brighton's coat of arms. A consequence of the agreement was that BH&D operated 11 trolleybuses, the only such vehicles in a Tilling fleet, on joint services from 1946 until 1959.

In September 1948 Brighton & Hove, together with the rest of the Tilling Group's bus operations, passed to the newly created British Transport Commission. In 1963 the company became a part of the Transport Holding Company, which had been formed as part of a reorganisation of the state-owned transport sector.

The post-war years saw large local authority housing estates built at Bevendean, Coldean and Moulsecoomb, all of which were served by the buses of BET-owned Southdown Motor Services, a situation that was heavily criticised by members of the local council and public alike, as its buses did not serve the main shopping areas of Brighton,

Thomas Tilling started operating buses in Brighton in 1916. In 1932, three years before operations were renamed Brighton & Hove, two AEC Regents are seen the centre of Brighton. (AEC)

Brighton & Hove built up a large fleet of highbridge ECW-bodied Bristol KSWs. 6447 (HAP 985) was acquired by the present-day company from a preservationist in 1986 and is still used on special services throughout the year.

terminating instead at the Pool Valley bus station located near the Palace Pier. To address this it was suggested that the joint agreement between the council and BH&D should be renegotiated to include Southdown, although little happened until January 1961 when a new pooling arrangement came into effect. The Brighton Area Transport Services (BATS), in which BH&D took 50.5% of revenue, Southdown 29% and the Corporation 20.5%, saw fares, ticketing and conditions of carriage standardised and routes reallocated between the three partners whilst BATS took a share of Southdown's revenue on longer-distance services. Southdown retained its separate identity with green and cream buses and fleetname, whilst "Brighton Corporation" was adopted as a fleetname by the municipal fleet, although its vehicles continued to carry red and cream livery.

With the formation of the National Bus Company on 1 January 1969, Brighton, Hove & District was merged with Southdown. The combined operation had a 79.5% share of BATS revenue and mileage. Although a discreet BH&D identity was retained for a while, the combined fleet soon began appearing in Southdown's apple-green livery, which was replaced by NBC leaf green from late 1972. Early repaints carried a Southdown-BH&D fleetname although the "BH&D" suffix was soon dropped. Brighton Corporation adopted a blue and white livery in 1970 and, following local government reorganisation in 1974, rebranded itself as Brighton Borough Transport.

Brighton & Hove's early fleet was somewhat London-centric and AECs predominated. Its 11 trolleybuses were a mixture of AEC 661Ts and similar BUT 9611Ts with bodywork built by Weymann. Its post-war bus fleet was largely made up of ECW-bodied Bristols, as would be expected from a BTC company. Unlike most BTC companies, however, low bridges were not a serious operational issue and large numbers of highbridge bodied Bristol K family vehicles were delivered during the 1940s and 50s. Brighton & Hove was a relatively late convert to the Bristol Lodekka although it did take significant numbers of the relatively uncommon 27ft front-entrance FSF model. Double-deckers dominated the fleet, the only exceptions in the post-war period being a batch of 10 Bristol RESLs delivered in 1969.

Southdown was one of the larger NBC operating companies and, as a prelude to deregulation and privatisation, its Brighton and Hove-area services had been transferred into a separate division in March 1985 pending a formal split

The National Bus Company amalgamated Brighton & Hove's operations with those of neighbouring Southdown, in whose green livery the combined fleet was painted. For a short while the new operation carried "Southdown-BH&D" fleetnames, as shown by 2021 (SPM 21) seen in Patcham during November 1972. (Dale Tringham)

Brighton Corporation painted its buses in the same red and cream livery as Brighton & Hove until 1970, when the municipal fleet adopted blue and white. Resting at Old Steine in October 1976 is 23 (23 ACD), a 1963 Leyland PD3 with Weymann bodywork. (Tony Wilson)

of the company. On 1 January 1986 the Brighton, Hove & District company was reactivated and assumed control of these services. The revived operation was renamed "Brighton & Hove Bus and Coach Company" on 21 April that year. Another significant change in the run-up to deregulation was the ending of BATS in January 1986, as such arrangements were incompatible with a competitive environment in which bus operators were expected to actively attract passengers from their rivals and operate in a commercial fashion.

The new company developed a fresh identity with a red, cream and black livery finished off by an attractively styled "Brighton & Hove" fleetname. Although early sales of NBC subsidiaries attracted relatively few bidders, interest quickly built up and, by the time Brighton & Hove was sold to its management team on 8 May 1987 there were three other parties expressing interest in the company, whose assets were valued at £2.8 million.

In common with other NBC companies there had been few new vehicles in recent years, partly as a result of the ending of the new bus grant and also because of the scarcity of funds in the run-up to privatisation. The new operation inherited 213 vehicles from Southdown, mainly typical NBC fare such as Leyland Nationals and Bristol VRTs, together with a small number of Park Royal-bodied Leyland Atlanteans which were disposed of fairly quickly. The company quickly established itself in the former Brighton, Hove & District head office and garage in Conway Street, Hove, and also assumed control of the Southdown depots at Freshfield Road, Whitehawk Road and Moulsecoomb Way in Brighton.

Brighton & Hove recognised the importance of investing in fleet replacement to address the legacy of an elderly, unattractive fleet inherited from the National Bus Company. The newly independent company was free to make its own decisions on vehicle policy and, after evaluating what was then available, bought 30 East Lancs-bodied Scanias between 1988 and 1990. Further arrivals in 1990 were a batch of 19 Wadham Stringer-bodied Mercedes-Benz 811D minibuses that had been delivered to Bournemouth Transport the previous year but not found favour. They lasted somewhat longer in their new home, the last not being withdrawn until March 2001.

The economic recession in the late 1980s and early 1990s had a significant effect on south-east England and passenger numbers fell by almost 9% between 1990 and 1991, and by 10% between 1991 and 1992. This coincided with a period of significantly increasing costs which required efficiency savings including closure of the Freshfield Road depot, shedding of non-operational posts and halting investment in fleet replacement. Although the period saw relatively few new vehicles purchased Brighton & Hove realised that in order to secure really good terms from suppliers it was preferable to negotiate as part of a larger organisation. Along with a number of other ex-NBC companies, it was a shareholder in South East Bus Investments Ltd (SEBIL) which sought to make bulk purchase and help fund other acquisitions.

By the 1990s the bus industry was beginning to consolidate. This was the result of a number of factors including the desire by some of the original buy-out teams to realise the value of their investment and the expansionist policies being pursued by some of the newly emerging transport groups.

In respect of Brighton & Hove a number of considerations led the management team to seek a buyer in 1993. The recession meant that trading conditions were still quite harsh and two of the founding directors were looking to retire. In addition, Stagecoach, the highly acquisitive Scottish bus operator, was raising its profile in the region, having acquired Southdown from its management buy-out team in August 1989. The growing dominance of Stagecoach convinced the directors that an approach to that organisation to purchase Brighton & Hove would almost certainly attract the adverse attention of the competition authorities. Another potential suitor, Badgerline, formed out of the sale of Bristol Omnibus's rural services, was in the throes of floating itself on the Stock Exchange

Brighton & Hove took delivery of 30 new East Lancs-bodied Scanias between 1988 and 1990, setting a pattern for new vehicle deliveries that endured for over two decades. Shortly after delivery 702 (E702 EFG) is seen near Gatwick Airport. (Chris Jones)

which was occupying most of its management resources. Approaches were therefore made to GRT Holdings, which was in the process of making its first acquisitions outside of its Scottish base, and Go-Ahead Northern.

The offers made by both companies were broadly comparable, but in the end the directors accepted an offer of £5 million from Go-Ahead Northern and, on 17 November 1993, Brighton & Hove became its first acquisition outside the north-east of England. Although a number of factors will have influenced the final outcome, it is clear that the buyer's clearly stated policy of allowing its subsidiary companies to operate relatively free of what can often be seen as corporate interference played a part. The acquisition was particularly attractive to Go-Ahead Northern as it fitted in with the desire to expand into urban areas in the south of England.

Following acquisition by Go-Ahead, fleet renewal, which had been scaled back for financial reasons, resumed. A further 31 Scanias arrived between 1996 and 1999 with East Lancs' distinctive Cityzen body, the last of which left the fleet during 2010. In the mid-1990s the company took 20 of a large Go-Ahead Group order for Dennis Darts with Marshall bodywork along with 18 of the relatively rare Optare Sigma-bodied Dennis Lance.

Passenger growth since then has dictated the use of double-deckers on most commercial services, although a small single-deck fleet is required primarily for routes that penetrate housing estates where parked cars can be an issue. It is also necessary to have a small pool of single-deckers for use on stormy days when double-deck vehicles cannot operate on the exposed coastal route to Eastbourne.

In addition to helping fund new vehicles, the new owners' access to finance also saw the acquisition in May 1997 of the 83-vehicle Brighton Blue Bus, the former arm's-length operation set up by Brighton Borough Council to run its bus services. Brighton Blue Bus had been sold to its management and employees in 1993 with a three-year clawback provision effectively preventing further sale during this period. The company had received approaches from Stagecoach prior to its sale to Go-Ahead for £5.76 million. Although initially retained as a separate entity, its operations were fully integrated with those of Brighton & Hove from 28 July 1997.

Brighton Corporation bought AEC-built buses and trolleybuses between 1939 and 1950, then Leylands mainly from 1959. Its first single-deckers were seven Leyland Panther Cubs new in 1968, the last of only 94 built. In the 1980s it operated three of the only four Bedford JJL midibuses. The fleet which passed to Go-Ahead ownership was still very heavily biased towards Leyland products, with Atlanteans, Nationals and Lynxes all featuring. Its most recent purchases, however, had been Dennis Darts in both step-entrance and low-floor variations.

The former municipal operator's premises in Lewes Road were also acquired and continue in use as an operational garage. The profile of Stagecoach's operations in the area helped ensure that the purchase was cleared

Brighton & Hove received 20 Marshall-bodied Dennis Darts during 1995, part of a larger order by the Go-Ahead Group. Showing the simpler livery adopted that year is 5 (N505 KCD).

by the Office of Fair Trading, whilst Brighton & Hove secured backing from local authorities, MPs and the public by promising to develop an integrated network for the area.

This new network manifested itself later in 1997 as "Metro", a colour-coded network covering five key routes that account for over half of the company's business. Metro built on the introduction in 1995 of route branding with colour-coded liveries by delivering improved frequencies, new vehicles and improved marketing. A simple Underground-style map was developed to overcome passengers' traditional reluctance to use bus maps. Whilst the shape of the Metro network has remained unchanged, frequencies have been enhanced as passenger numbers have grown.

Brighton & Hove also provides a commercial 24-hour, seven-day-a-week operation on Metro 7, linking Hove with Brighton Marina, and Metro 25 which serves the universities. These were introduced in 2004 and 2006 respectively, although night-bus operations date back to 1993 when a contracted service was introduced on behalf of the University of Sussex. Commercial operations started with a weekend operation in 1996 which was gradually expanded. In addition to the nightly operations within the city there are weekend services to Eastbourne, Uckfield, Worthing and Steyning reflecting Brighton & Hove's position as an entertainment centre.

Brighton Blue Bus's experience of low-floor single-deck operation prompted Brighton & Hove to take a batch of 21 Wright Renown-bodied Volvo B10BLEs in 1998 although, with the advent of low-floor double-deck buses these proved to be the last single-deckers to arrive for some time.

Brighton & Hove was an early customer for low-floor double-deckers; however, with no suitable offering from Scania, it was Dennis, with its Trident, that met the requirement. A total of 76 vehicles, 40 with East Lancs Lolyne bodies and 36 with the Plaxton President, were delivered between 1999 and 2002. Two of the East Lancs-bodied buses were built with convertible open-top bodies, the first low-floor buses so constructed. The level of investment meant that by the summer of 2000 the last survivors of the NBC era had been withdrawn.

The introduction of the low-floor East Lancs-bodied Omnidekka allowed Brighton & Hove to return to Scania as a chassis builder in 2003 and a total of 108 of this type joined the fleet, two of which have convertible bodies. More recently, 31 integral Scania OmniCity double-deckers and seven single-deckers have joined the fleet.

The need for smaller buses on some services is met by a number of Dennis Dart MPDs and a single Optare Solo acquired from Metrobus.

Notable additions to the fleet in 2010 were four articulated Mercedes-Benz Citaro artics, displaced from Red Arrow services in London. They are primarily used on the Metro 25 University service which experiences heavy tidal peak flows. They are also used on the extensive Park and Ride operations in connection with the new Community Stadium at Falmer opened in 2011, where their ability to carry nearly 150 passengers is particularly useful.

The dominance of Scania products in the fleet does not mean, however, that the company is not prepared to evaluate other types, and short-term loans, particularly from fellow Go-Ahead companies, are not unusual. Such loans are generally used in service and have included one of London General's Alexander Dennis Enviro400H

The company's first low-floor double-deckers arrived during 1999. In the absence of a low-floor product from Scania, the chassis choice was Dennis's Trident. Shortly after delivery 806 (T806 RFG) passes through Palmeira Square, Hove.

hybrid double-deckers. Since 2011 the company has received 39 Wright Eclipse Gemini 2-bodied Volvo B9TLs, part of a Group-wide order that saw similar vehicles delivered to Go North East and London. Two Volvo B5LH hybrid buses, previously used as demonstrators by Volvo, joined the fleet during early 2012; these will be followed later in the year by 11 similar vehicles, partly funded by the government's Green Bus Fund. These buses will be used on Metro service 7 and the inter-urban route 28 linking Brighton and Lewes, thus allowing an assessment of their impact on two routes with different characteristics and operating conditions.

A small private-hire fleet, which is a familiar sight throughout south-east England and beyond, is maintained. In addition to charter work, a range of tours and excursions is offered, many of which are actively promoted by the company's in-house publications.

Brighton & Hove has always been aware of its heritage and two historic vehicles are retained which are available for weddings and corporate hires, as well as appearing occasionally in service and attending bus rallies. ECW-bodied Bristol KSW6G 6447 was reacquired from private preservation in 1986 and restored to pre-NBC Tilling red and cream livery, while former London AEC/Park Royal Routemaster RML2317 joined the fleet in 2009 from Metrobus. It is painted in a representation of Tilling livery, partly in recognition of its London links but also to depict the company's pre-1935 identity.

The 1995 delivery of Dennis Darts introduced a new, simplified livery which still retained the same basic colour palette of red, cream and black. It was subsequently adapted to allow for colour-coded route branding with the red being replaced. Early 2004 saw the adoption of a contemporary style, still based upon the same three colours, developed by Best Impressions. The new brand was accompanied by the end of commercial advertising from third parties in favour of promotional messages designed to raise the profile of bus travel.

The first of these was the "I'm on the bus" campaign in which prominent local people, whose images appeared supersized on the side of vehicles, explained why they were proud to use Brighton & Hove buses. The scheme was hugely popular and was subsequently extended to include colleagues who work for Brighton & Hove across the full range of different jobs that go to make up the company. Even Managing Director Roger French appeared on one to thank everyone for their support. In 2009 the company launched its "Bus & the City" campaign which saw vehicles carrying a range of messages extolling the virtues of its services, exploiting the ampersand in its fleetname.

Although route branding is still carried on some buses, all vehicles now carry a similar red and cream livery with the branding restricted to a coloured swoop and vinyls describing the individual route. The rear of most vehicles carries promotional messages designed to articulate the positive attributes of bus travel or highlight the more negative aspects of car use.

Since 1999, Brighton & Hove's buses have been named after notable deceased people with a connection to the area. The idea originated as the first double-deck low-floor buses were due to be delivered, and every new bus that has entered the fleet since has been named. The main criterion for inclusion is that the deceased person made a

Brighton & Hove buses do not carry commercial advertising, instead using the space to promote bus use. In January 2005 the company launched its "I'm on the bus" campaign in which local people provided their endorsement.

Brighton & Hove is noted for the quality of its publicity. Since 1987 it has published *Bus Times*, a twice-yearly publication providing timetables of its own services and those of other operators, together with other useful information. Its artistic cover photographs have also become something of note.

significant contribution to the area or had a strong connection during their lifetime. As more contemporary names have been suggested, another criteria is that the person has been deceased for at least a year.

Brighton & Hove has been experiencing a growth in passenger numbers since 1993, when it reversed 35 years of declining patronage. The area is good bus-operating territory – it is densely populated, with a wide socio-economic mix including large numbers of students; traffic congestion along key main routes can be significant and it has retained a vibrant central area which can be well served by bus. Crucially, it also has a sympathetic local authority keen to develop public transport usage.

A combination of innovative marketing and local authority support have helped ensure that Brighton & Hove, and Roger French, its hands-on Managing Director, are well known both to industry insiders and the wider public. Roger was part of the original team that bought the company out from NBC and became MD at the time of sale to Go-Ahead. He has pioneered a number of initiatives, since mimicked elsewhere, based upon a simple formula. Key to this is frequency with most services, including the inter-urban coastal service linking Brighton and Eastbourne, running at least every ten minutes. Service levels on Sundays and public holidays (including Boxing Day and New Year's Day) are still high. This ensures that timetables become irrelevant and helps to attract the casual user whilst real-time bus-stop information also helps reassure passengers that the bus is not far away.

In addition to growth on the established network, further expansion saw Brighton & Hove acquire Stagecoach's operations centred on Lewes in September 2005, including services to Tunbridge Wells and Uckfield together with the remaining share of the previously jointly-operated routes linking Brighton and Eastbourne. It acquired 15 Dennis buses (seven Tridents, five Lance SLFs and three Darts) as part of the deal, although the Lances were disposed of relatively quickly.

In the summer of 2008 Eastbourne Borough Council announced that it was to sell Eastbourne Buses, its loss-making operation that was heir to the world's first municipal bus service. Although Go-Ahead, through Brighton & Hove, submitted a proposal which was clearly favoured by the undertaking's staff and would have learned from the successful integration of Brighton Blue Buses, Stagecoach bid significantly more for the business.

The latest promotional campaign makes use of the ampersand in the company's name to advertise the advantages of bus travel. Scania OmniCity 729 (YP09 HWS) extols the virtues of Brighton & Hove's high-frequency services.

Above left: Metro 25, linking the universities of Brighton and Sussex with the city centre, experiences particularly heavy peak loadings. During 2009 four Mercedes-Benz Citaro articulated buses joined the fleet. Further similar vehicles arrived during 2011, allowing the entire service to be converted to this mode of operation.

Above right: Since 2012 Brighton & Hove has taken delivery of 39 Wright Eclipse 2-bodied Volvo B9TLs. George Street, Hove, is the setting for 405 (BJ11 XHE) seen adjacent to a local authority-provided "next bus" display.

Brighton & Hove is also noted for its simple, well-publicised fare system which also helps dispel the myth that bus travel is expensive. There are just three levels of fare for most journeys within the city: short hop, centrefare and standard. The company also recognises that family trips by bus may appear disproportionately more expensive by bus than by car. The bus ID scheme, available to all children aged from 5-19 residing in the city, allows them to travel for as little as 20 pence. A range of saver tickets is available for multiple journeys, covering time periods of one day to an annual season ticket. Although the shorter-validity tickets are available from bus drivers, there are price incentives to obtain them in advance, whether from a network of commercial partners or via the company's website.

Effective marketing and a modern fleet are also essential components of Brighton & Hove's success. Sustained investment has delivered a 100% fully accessible fleet with no vehicle over 13 years old. Low-floor buses have revolutionised the accessibility of public transport for a wide range of customers, from the elderly who are uneasy at tackling steps through to mothers with buggies and small children. For wheelchair users they have opened up a whole new world of independent travel previously unavailable.

As already noted, buses do not carry commercial advertising, instead using the space available to market the virtues of bus travel (or highlight the perils of car use). This is supported by *Bus Times*, an attractively-produced magazine that combines timetable information for all pubic transport within the company's operating area (including rail services and those provided by other operators) with useful guides to how to use the bus and suggestions for days out. *Bus Times* is published twice a year and distributed free of charge across a wide area. Since its launch in 1987 it has gained a strong following and is particularly noted for the artistic photography on its front cover! Good quality printed media are supplemented by an attractive, intuitively-designed website that provides up-to-date travel information and a wealth of detail on the company's history, its fleet and the background to the names carried on its buses. Two travel shops, branded "1 Stop Travel", are also maintained at Old Steine, near the Royal Pavilion, and in the city's main railway station. In addition to supplying information in respect of Brighton & Hove services, these also provide a booking service for National Express coach services, rail tickets and the company's programme of excursions.

An ingrained customer-services ethos is also vital. This has to apply to all staff in the organisation who must understand that not only does the customer have a choice but that just one unfortunate experience may well deter them from coming back. Although drivers are obviously at the sharp end, everyone in the team has an equally important role to play, with managers travelling regularly by bus to ensure that they have a real feel for the product being offered. It is also essential that staff are kept fully informed of developments affecting their company, rather than finding things out from the local press. With this in mind a fortnightly newsletter, *infolink*, is produced containing general updates about all elements of the business.

A final component of Brighton & Hove's success story is the support of its local authority. Brighton & Hove Council was created as a unitary body in 1997 with city status following in 2000. The council recognises the rôle that effective bus services have in delivering a more attractive urban environment and has provided well-designed bus stops with waiting shelters and real-time information; it has also ensured that parking restrictions and bus lanes are rigorously enforced and additionally manages the city's park-and-ride car park. Unusually, all of this is achieved without the need to introduce a formal partnership of any sort, a situation that demonstrates the level of mutual respect and trust which exists between the city and its local bus operator. A crucial element in building this trust is the fact that Roger French and his team are seen as integral to the local community, an arrangement that is encouraged by Go-Ahead's policy of empowering its managers to develop solutions appropriate to their local areas.

Chapter 5

Oxford Bus Company
Innovation, competition and partnership

The Oxford Bus Company traces its origins to the establishment of the City of Oxford and District Tramways Company Limited, which started operating a horse-drawn tramway service from the town's railway station to Cowley Road in 1881. The system expanded quickly and by the early years of the twentieth century it was proposed that the network should be electrified, although local opposition to the erection of overhead cables on historic buildings prevented the works being taken forward.

In 1905 the tramway's owners offered to sell the system to Oxford City Council. Local resistance to public funding led the council to buy the tramway but seek tenders for its operation. The contract to provide services was awarded to the National Electric Construction Company from 1907, which established the City of Oxford Electric Tramway Ltd.

The Council required that NEC investigate the potential to electrify the network without the use of overhead wires. Although use of a system using metal studs to carry traction current was considered, this had proved unsafe and unreliable elsewhere and was not pursued.

The absence of a viable means of electrifying the tramway network forced consideration of other alternatives to the increasingly anachronistic horse trams and the company proposed that motor buses should be introduced, although this was initially opposed by the council. William Morris, the owner of the eponymous motor manufacturer based in the city, decided to force the issue by starting his own motor bus services in December 1913. Whether it was intended or not, Morris's actions led to the council dropping its opposition to motor bus services being operated by the tramway company. Services were introduced within three weeks of Morris's operations and the motor magnate promptly sold his buses to the established operator. Withdrawal of the tramway services followed quickly.

The City of Oxford fleet featured a large proportion of AECs. The Oxford Bus Museum's preserved Park Royal-bodied AEC Regent V 956 (956 AJO) is seen leaving the historic Cowley Road garage for the last time on 19 September 2004.

City of Oxford's initial rear-engined double deckers were Daimler Fleetlines. Northern Counties-bodied 426 shows the simpler "Oxford" fleetname reinstated after many of the rural services were passed to a newly re-established South Midland in advance of privatisation. (Author's collection)

The Oxford Electric Tramways Act 1914 granted the company the right to run motor buses in Oxford for 37 years for a rent to the council of £800 a year. Additional services were started to surrounding towns, commencing with one to Abingdon in 1914. Although further development was arrested by the Great War, the early years of peace saw rapid expansion take place and in 1921 the company assumed the title of City of Oxford Motor Services Ltd.

Services had initially been operated from a depot in Leopold Street; however, by 1924 this was proving inadequate and a new garage was built in Cowley Road, which remained the company's main operational base and headquarters until September 2004. Further expansion saw operating bases established in a number of surrounding towns and villages including Stokenchurch, Thame, Witney, Bicester and Wantage, whilst links were established to new housing developments in the city.

In 1930 the Great Western Railway acquired a 49% stake in the company, whilst the following year NEC was taken over by BET. Nationalisation of the railways in 1948 saw the GWR's shareholding pass to the British Transport Commission. In 1968, along with BET's other bus-operating interests, City of Oxford found itself as part of the newly established National Bus Company.

The NBC quickly set about rationalising the number of operators in its portfolio by amalgamating neighbouring concerns. In January 1971 City of Oxford therefore assumed control of South Midland Motor Services. South Midland had been purchased by Red & White in 1945. Red & White then sold its operations to the British Transport Commission in 1950 which had placed the South Midland operation under the control of its Thames Valley subsidiary. The business brought with it control of the express coach services between London and Oxford that had been initiated in 1927. The fleetname displayed on buses, which had hitherto been "Oxford" was changed to "Oxford – South Midland" to reflect the newly enlarged operation.

Further changes saw the company's livery, which had been red, maroon and duck-egg green until the late 1960s (when the maroon was abandoned) replaced by NBC corporate poppy red from late 1972. Interestingly, however, when the National Express coach network was established, bringing with it the now familiar white coaches, the service between London and Oxford was not included. It was operated under a road service licence rather than an express service licence, and therefore retained its own identity.

Environmental concerns have long been an issue in Oxford and the company launched an experimental electric bus service in the city during 1994. One of the vehicles is seen being recharged at Oxford station during June. (Tony Wilson)

Acquisition of The Bee Line's High Wycombe operations brought a large number of elderly vehicles into the fleet, including Leyland Nationals. Showing the revised livery adopted after privatisation is 1321 (TBL 165M). Vehicles in Oxford carried Oxford Bus Company fleetnames.

Under BET control City of Oxford had considerable freedom to make its own fleet policy and standardised on AECs. Although five Dennis Lolines joined the fleet in 1961, even these had AEC engines. With the advent of rear-engined double-deckers a number of Daimler Fleetlines arrived, both new and second-hand examples from other NBC subsidiaries. From 1973 to 1981 all new double-deckers were Bristol VRTs with Eastern Coach Works bodies. Meanwhile, a small number of ex-London Transport DMS buses had been acquired in 1979. These were followed by Leyland Olympians, largely to replace Fleetlines.

Although single-deck buses formed a small proportion of the fleet, a number of ECW-bodied Bristol REs were operated and, for lightly loaded rural routes, Duple Dominant-bodied Ford R1014s. In the early 1980s City of Oxford took delivery of a fleet of Ford Transit minibuses for use on services where larger vehicles could not operate. These services were ultimately branded "Nipper" and carried a green, white and blue livery. MCW Metroriders replaced the Transits.

Oxford has a restricted central area with many historic buildings, and a river crossing between the central area and the main residential areas in the city. As the use of private transport grew during the 1960s, it was accepted that some way of managing transport demand had to be found other than simply building new roads.

In 1968 the city and county councils commissioned a report into the city's future transport needs which led, in 1973, to the adoption of a Balanced Transport Plan (BTP). This plan sought to contain and reduce the use of private transport within the Oxford ring road, by encouraging the use of public transport, cycling and walking. Importantly, the strategy contained measures to discourage car use, mainly by the pricing and availability of car parking. In addition, the two main central shopping streets, Cornmarket Street and Queen Street were closed to traffic other than buses.

The plan also saw the creation of the first permanent park-and-ride site in the UK, at Redbridge to the south of the city. A further four park-and-ride sites have since been established, making the Oxford park-and-ride system one of the largest of its type in the UK.

Further evidence of the local authority's commitment to environmentally-friendly transport was its support, in conjunction with Southern Electric, of the "City Circuit" service linking the railway station to the Oxford Science

What was still the Go-Ahead Northern Group acquired City of Oxford in 1994. The first new vehicles delivered were a batch of 20 Marshall-bodied Dennis Darts which carried a new livery and Cityline fleetnames. 519 (M519 VJO) is seen at Oxford station when new.

Although seven early low-floor Dennis Darts joined the Wycombe Bus fleet in 1996, the first low-floor buses for Oxford were a batch of 10 Wright Crusader-bodied Dennis Darts delivered in 1998. Showing the revised Oxford Bus Company fleetname introduced in 2000 is 410 (R410 FFC).

Park. The service, launched in 1994, used two battery-powered Metroriders. Operation passed to Thames Transit in 1997 and the service was withdrawn, due to lack of funding, in 1998.

In advance of deregulation and privatisation of the NBC many of the larger subsidiaries were divided into smaller units. This saw most of City of Oxford's rural operations pass to a re-created South Midland in June 1984. In addition to the urban network a number of services, including those to Reading and Aylesbury, were retained by City of Oxford, which reverted to displaying "Oxford" as a fleetname.

Deregulation in 1986 saw little outward change and most of City of Oxford's services were registered to be run commercially. All this changed from March 1987 when Thames Transit, founded by Harry Blundred who had purchased Devon General from the NBC and had previously been Traffic Manager at City of Oxford, commenced services in competition with City of Oxford, linking the large Blackbird Leys estate with the city centre using 16-seater minibuses. An express service to London, branded "Oxford Tube", was also introduced. Thames Transit also acquired South Midland, which had been sold to its management team, in 1989 and introduced further services in competition with City of Oxford.

City of Oxford was sold to its management team, led by Arthur Townsend, on 15 January 1987. The new owners quickly introduced a new livery, in this case of dark red with a black skirt and white roof, and adopted Oxford Bus Company (OBC) as a fleetname.

In November 1990 the 51-strong High Wycombe operations of the Berks Bucks Bus Company (the Bee Line) were acquired and rebranded as Wycombe Bus Company, vehicles carrying the same livery as the Oxford fleet.

By late 1993 the Directors of OBC were seeking to sell the operation which, although profitable, had begun to suffer from the increasing competitive assault by Thames Transit. Although initial discussions had taken place with Western Travel, which itself was subsequently sold to Stagecoach, the business was sold to Go-Ahead Northern on 1 March 1994 for £6.3 million.

The new management team, led by former Go-Ahead Gateshead manager Keith Moffatt, quickly sought to improve the image of the company, which was operating an increasingly elderly fleet and had become unable to respond effectively to competition. It was recognised, however, that the market for bus travel in the city was strong, the route network was comprehensive and that the company had loyal, committed staff.

The new Go-Ahead team sought to refresh OBC's image. It was recognised that the company's name was a particular strength, being seen as a well-established local brand. Crucially, this also sat comfortably with the Go-Ahead ethos that its bus operations should be managed locally and seen as part of the community that they serve.

The result was adoption of a slightly amended fleetname, "the Oxford Bus Company" with a stylised "dreaming spires" logo. Discreet brand names were employed for each of the three groups of service operated, Cityline for local bus services, Citylink for the express coach services to London and Park & Ride. The Cityline fleet adopted a red, white and blue livery which was also adopted for services operated by Wycombe Bus. At the same time a

Oxford was the first city in the UK with a permanent park-and-ride site, opened in 1973. In 1999 the Park & Ride fleet was upgraded by the arrival of 20 Alexander-bodied Dennis Tridents the arrival of which coincided with the launch of the Oxford Transport Strategy. Brand-new 106 (T106 DBW) is seen at the Thornhill Park & Ride site on 10 July 1999.

review of services led to the remaining inter-urban routes being withdrawn to allow the company to focus on urban services within Oxford itself.

Cityline services retained a red-based livery, initially with a blue skirt (replacing the previous black) and white roof. In recent years, this has been updated to a two-tone red livery which matches modern bus styles, and the brand name has developed into "city" with the latest branding exercise playing on "city" to create promotional slogans such as "capa-city", "viva-city", and "elasti-city".

Park & Ride had come to be viewed almost as a second-rate service with elderly vehicles (including rebodied coaches) carrying all-over advertising. Under Go-Ahead ownership, the strategic importance of Park & Ride was recognised and a highly visible lime green, blue and white livery adopted with appropriate promotional messages. With successive batches of new buses, the "green" theme has developed further so that it is now a deep green shade.

The coach fleet maintained a version of the blue-based NBC coach livery, initially under the generic brand of "Citylink". This changed in 2001 with the adoption of "the airline" as a discrete brand for services to Heathrow and Gatwick, whilst the London service from 2004 emerged as "oxford espress" carrying a green and orange livery applied in the same house style as that of "the airline". The coach services linking the city with Heathrow and Gatwick airports represent a market which has shown significant growth, proving popular with tourists, business travellers and airport workers. The initial hourly service to Heathrow has expanded to a coach every 20 minutes to Heathrow and hourly to Gatwick at busy times. Both "airline" and "oxford espress" coaches are replaced regularly and feature high-quality interiors, with low-density seating together with at-seat laptop-charging sockets reflecting the product's high-quality image. On-board wi-fi has also been provided and the services attract a significant number of business users who value the ability to work in comfort during their journey. During December 2012 "the airline" brand was refreshed and a fleet of 18 new Plaxton Panther-bodied Scania coaches introduced. This allowed the previous fleet to be refurbished for use on a new-look X90 Oxford-London service from 5 March 2012

Although the Balanced Transport Plan had been successful in containing the growth of car use within the ring road by the early 1990s, there was a feeling that the traffic situation in central Oxford needed to be addressed, changing the principle from containment to restraint. The Oxford Transport Strategy (OTS) was therefore developed with the aim of improving the quality of central-area shopping streets. To achieve this, Cornmarket Street was closed to buses and High Street closed to general traffic, with a Bus Priority Route created around the central area. As a result of OTS and other pro-public transport measures, 44% of people travelling into central Oxford now do so by bus.

Frequent coach services link Oxford with Heathrow and Gatwick airports. In 2001 these services were relaunched as the "airline". Seen entering Oxford is 83 (CB07 OXF), a Plaxton Panther-bodied Volvo B12 delivered 2007. As with most recent deliveries this vehicle has a cherished registration featuring "OXF".

In the mid-1990s a number of local authorities proposed reintroducing tramways as a means of encouraging people out of their cars. Given its history, such an initiative was highly unlikely to succeed in Oxford. The company therefore proposed development of a guided busway, largely using disused rail lines, initially linking the Pear Tree and Redbridge park-and-ride sites through the city centre. Although the Guided Transit Expressway was well received by local authorities it failed to secure government funding and was shelved. Managing director Keith Moffatt was particularly associated with this project which led directly to him being appointed Group Development Director with Go-Ahead in 1996, to be succeeded by Douglas Adie who had been Managing Director of London Central.

A significant step was taken in 1994 with the introduction of "Freedom" cards, season tickets which could be purchased from the driver and validated on-bus. This proved a great boost to market share in the competitive environment by guaranteeing customer loyalty. A spin-off from this was the introduction of one of the first local bus add-ons to rail tickets, in 1997.

The sale of Thames Transit to Stagecoach in 1997 brought a more mature approach to competition and helped lead to the launch of Plus + Pass in 1998, a season ticket valid between Oxford city centre and Kennington / Kidlington on services operated by Oxford Bus Company and Stagecoach. Its scope was subsequently expanded and a one-day version introduced. Unusually, the one-day ticket is actually issued for a period of 24 hours from the time of issue rather than for one calendar day.

In 2006, Oxford Bus introduced one of the first commercial smartcard systems in the UK, superseding the Freedom card range. Branded the "key", the smartcard now has over 36,000 customers and the concept is being extended across the remainder of the Go-Ahead Group – both rail and bus.

Following privatisation, the fleet was initially updated with new Optare MetroRiders, Alexander-bodied Leyland Olympians and 25 ex-London Leyland Titans, although the acquisition of Wycombe Bus worsened the age profile somewhat. The coach fleet also benefited from regular investment, with some of the older vehicles rebodied as buses using Willowbrook Warrior coachwork.

Early arrivals for fleet renewal under Go-Ahead ownership saw 20 of the Group's 1995 order for 120 Marshall-bodied Dennis Darts replace Bristol VRTs on some of the more lightly trafficked routes. These vehicles were the

Express services linking Oxford and Abingdon were introduced in 1996. In December 2003 a relaunch saw new Abingdon Direct-branded Mercedes-Benz Citaros introduced. The two-tone red livery was also adopted for the remainder of the Oxford network which began to use "city" branding.

The Oxford–London corridor is highly competitive and from early 2004 City of Oxford marketed its services as "oxford espress" with the emphasis very much on providing a relaxed way of travelling.

first in the Group to be fitted with Continuously Regenerating Trap exhaust systems which significantly reduced their emissions. In addition, seven Plaxton Pointer-bodied low-floor Darts, part funded by the local authority, were delivered to Wycombe. The Wycombe services were not, however, sufficiently profitable to support further investment in new vehicles, although the age profile was improved by transferring in mid-life vehicles from elsewhere.

In common with many other operators, Oxford Bus Company moved away from double-deckers during the 1990s. Following arrival of the Dennis Darts further renewal of the fleet was achieved by a large influx of Volvo B10B single-deckers. Initial deliveries of Plaxton Verde-bodied vehicles were followed by mid-life examples with Northern Counties bodies transferred from London General. The launch of Volvo's low-floor B10BLE chassis saw a batch of vehicles ordered with coachwork by Wright. These vehicles had dual-door bodywork, which was viewed as essential given the heavy loadings and simultaneous loading and disembarking that took place at city centre stops.

The spring of 1999 a saw a batch of 20 Alexander-bodied Dennis Tridents delivered for the park-and-ride services. These represented the first low-floor double-deckers in the fleet and were amongst the first for any operator outside London. Their arrival coincided with the launch of the Oxford Transport Strategy and demonstrated the operator's commitment to complementing initiatives taken by the local authority.

On 14 December 2000 the Wycombe Bus operation was sold to Arriva for £5m. Although passenger numbers had increased by 21% since its acquisition, the network was not sufficiently profitable to fund long-term fleet replacement. In addition, the local council intended to redevelop High Wycombe bus station which also housed the Wycombe Bus depot. As the only alternative site was next to Arriva's existing garage it was felt more appropriate to dispose of the operation and allow Arriva to develop an integrated network.

In 2001, Philip Kirk was appointed Managing Director, succeeding Douglas Adie who had retired. Philip had previously been Operations Manager and then Commercial Director with the company. As with sister companies

Success in winning the contract to provide BrookesBus, a network of services operated primarily for students and staff of Oxford Brookes University from the summer of 2009, saw 11 ADL Enviro400-bodied Scania double-deckers join the fleet. Heading past The Plain is 210 (KF10 OXF).

The streets of Oxford have seen high levels of competition between Oxford Bus Company and Stagecoach Oxford. In 2010 both operators, together with the local authority, unveiled the latest stage in the Transform Oxford strategy which included the introduction of co-ordinated timetables and ticketing on four key routes into the city centre. Both operators introduced new double-deck vehicles and Oxford Bus Company's 231 (MF10 OXF) shows off the current branding for city services as it heads along Park End Street.

in the group, the OBC team is well connected in the community through participation and leadership in chambers of commerce and city-centre management organisations.

In December 2002 the city's fifth park-and-ride facility opened at Water Eaton, with bus services provided by a fleet of five Mercedes-Benz Citaros in a revised livery of three shades of green.

The company's depot at Cowley Road was in need of significant improvements to meet modern requirements and, although consideration was given to rebuilding on the existing site, it was clear that any planning application would only be granted with restrictions: the city had grown up around the site which was now in a residential area. A new facility was built on part of the former Morris site in Cowley and opened in 2004. The choice of location was influenced in large part by a desire to minimise the impact on staff, many of whom lived on the south side of the city.

Oxford is surrounded by a green belt in which new housing development is heavily restricted. This has led to the development of a number of dormitory towns, most notably Abingdon, which have grown significantly in recent years. Although many people commuted to Oxford, bus services had tended to follow historical routes through a number of villages and were relatively slow. In 1996 OBC introduced the X3, an express service which followed a direct route into the city. The initial 20-minute frequency has been increased incrementally to a bus every six minutes during the peak periods and, in December 2003, new Mercedes-Benz Citaros replaced the Volvo B10Bs previously used. This upgrade enhanced the profile of the service, and it is noteworthy that many passengers view it as more akin to a train service than a bus and are prepared to walk up to one mile to join the service.

On 1 July 2009 the Oxford Bus Company took over the operation of BrookesBus from Stagecoach Oxford, which had operated it since its inception, having won a five-year contract. The services, which comprise two routes operated on behalf of Oxford Brookes University, link its campuses in Headington, North Hinksey and

Thames Travel, acquired by Go-Ahead in May 2011, operates in south Oxfordshire and east Berkshire. Passing though Wallingford, where the operation is based, is 108 (AE08 DLD), an MCV Evolution-bodied ADL Dart.

The Oxford Bus Company's fleet is one of the most environmentally friendly in the United Kingdom. In the summer of 2011 its green credentials were reinforced when the entire Park & Ride fleet was replaced with 17 ADL Enviro400H hybrid buses carrying a striking new livery. The first of the batch, with an appropriate registration mark, is seen at Pear Tree Park & Ride.

Wheatley and carry around 1.7 million passengers per annum. Although contracted by the university, the services are available to members of the general public as well as students and university staff, and are seen as an integral contributor to reducing the number of cars on its campuses. Eleven ADL Enviro400-bodied Scania double-deckers were acquired for the services. The buses, which have leather seats, air-conditioning and wi-fi facilities, are finished in a dark blue livery. Such has been the success of this service that the initial fleet was quickly augmented by a further nine vehicles cascaded from the park-and-ride service.

Whilst the years since 1987 have seen sporadic competition in a number of British towns and cities Oxford has been one of the few urban areas where there has been sustained competition between two major bus operators on a number of key corridors. Whilst this has undoubtedly led to better levels of service for passengers, there has been criticism of the sheer numbers of buses passing though the city centre. Although the local authority is supportive of public transport, there was a risk that public pressure might have forced it to take measures that would severely restrict access for all traffic, including buses, to the city centre to the detriment of both visitors and business. In early 2010 OBC and Oxfordshire County Council, together with Stagecoach, unveiled the Transform Oxford strategy to deliver a better environment for pedestrians in the city.

The new arrangement uses powers provided by the Local Transport Act 2008 to enable more effective partnership working between local authorities and bus operators to deliver co-ordinated bus services. Its launch in July 2011 saw both operators introduce integrated, "turn-up-and-go" high-frequency services on four key routes into the city, supported by an integrated smartcard ticketing system, allowing passengers to use either company's services with the same ticket. In advance of its launch single-decker vehicles were replaced by new, low-emission double-deckers, in OBC's case 20 new Scania double-deckers similar to those in use on the BrookesBus contract.

In May 2011 the park-and-ride fleet was refreshed with the introduction of 17 ADL Enviro400H hybrid buses part-funded by the Government's Green Bus scheme. During 2012 a further 19 hybrid buses will join the fleet, bringing the proportion of such vehicles up to 31% – one of the highest in the country. These buses, Volvo B5LHs with Wrightbus bodywork, will be used on city services, meaning that the operator will meet the city council's target for low-emission vehicles ahead of schedule.

During the winter of 2011/12 the Oxford Bus Company refreshed the brands used by its coach services linking Oxford with London and its airports. Newly delivered 12 (MF61 OXF) in "the airline" livery leads Oxford–London X90-branded 97 (GG08 OXF) out of Oxford.

In March 2012 High Wycombe-based Carousel Buses was acquired by the Go-Ahead Group. Delivered shortly before the takeover was a trio of MCV-bodied Mercedes OC500LF, one of which is seen near Gerrards Cross on the operator's popular service to Heathrow Airport.

Oxford Bus Company operates one of the most environmentally-friendly bus fleets anywhere in Britain and has been at the forefront of moves to improve air quality in Oxford, going above and beyond what is expected. To this end it has introduced a star rating system on its buses, based on independent standards set by the European Environment Agency, and is comfortably on target to meet the standards for the Oxford Low Emission Zone which will be introduced in 2013. In addition, it pioneered the use of the RIBAS (Revving, Idling, Braking, Acceleration and Speed) system in which in-cab prompts alert drivers when they are not driving in an efficient way. All drivers have been trained to exploit the potential of this technology, which has resulted in a 5% saving in fuel consumption together with a reduction in accidents as a result of a more sensitive driving style.

Go-Ahead acquired Wallingford-based Thames Travel during May 2011. Founded in 1998 by John Wright, who had previously managed Wright's of Wrexham, it had grown steadily and taken over a number of services previously provided by other operators that have ceased trading, notably Tillingbourne in 2001 and Chiltern Queens the following year. It also operates a number of services formerly provided by Stagecoach subsidiary Thames Transit which complemented its own network linking Wallingford with Reading, Oxford and Henley. In May 2010 it was successful in gaining a number of contracts for services in the Bracknell area.

Although Thames Travel buses were initially painted all-over white, an attractive green and blue livery was adopted in 2006. All vehicles are low-floor and include the first hybrid bus delivered to an independent operator.

As a result of passenger growth, particularly in the Wokingham area, and success in winning a number of local authority contracts in south Oxfordshire, additional fleet capacity was required during 2011. This has been met by transferring in a number of vehicles from the OBC fleet and that of Brighton & Hove.

On 3 March 2012 further growth saw Carousel Buses, based in High Wycombe, added to the Group's portfolio. Formed in August 2000 by Steve Burns and John Robinson, who had previously worked for local operators Classic Coaches and Abbey Coaches, Carousel initially focused on schools services and rail-replacement work. Subsequent expansion has seen the development of a network of tendered and commercial services throughout south Buckinghamshire with many of the latter having previously been operated by Arriva. Summer 2003 saw the launch of a service linking High Wycombe with Heathrow Airport, operated in partnership with Buckinghamshire County Council and Heathrow Airport Ltd. Subsequent development has seen a network of three routes introduced linking Chesham, High Wycombe, Uxbridge and the airport.

In its early days the fleet was dominated by Metrobuses, the majority of which had been new to London operators. More recently a mixture of new and mid-life low-floor vehicles have joined the fleet including examples of the relatively rare Irisbus AgoraLine and, in early 2012, the first MCV-bodied Mercedes-Benz OC500U to enter service with any operator. Go-Ahead moved swiftly to update the double-deck fleet by transferring Plaxton-bodied Volvo B7TL buses from London to replace the remaining Metrobuses.

Fleet livery was initially London red with white relief and a logo that bore more than a passing resemblance to that used by London Country in its early days. In 2004 a revised two-tone application was introduced; most vehicles carry red, although route-branded variations are used for some services.

These acquisitions complement OBC's established operations and, although continuing to operate as separate units, they share directors with OBC. Both retain their existing brand identities, although the fleets have been renumbered into a common series with the OBC fleet.

The Oxford Bus Company has secured three decades of passenger growth, contributing to ensuring that car use in Oxford, in defiance of trends elsewhere, continues to decline. The improved environment that this has brought has helped attract more people into the city and helped debunk the myth that by restricting car traffic local trade will be adversely affected.

Chapter 6

Go-Ahead London
Capital growth

London is a vast market for bus services, representing nearly half of all such journeys undertaken in the UK. Unlike the rest of Great Britain, bus services in London were not deregulated in 1986, although there was provision for this to happen.

The London Passenger Transport Board (LPTB – usually referred to by its operating name – London Transport) was established in 1933 to take control of most bus services, trams, trolleybuses and the Underground within a radius of about 30 miles from central London. Nationalisation in 1948 saw control pass to the British Transport Commission until this organisation was dissolved in 1963 whereupon it passed to a newly-created nationalised board. On 1 January 1970 the responsibility for most services within Greater London passed to the Greater London Council (GLC) whilst those operating outside this area were vested in the newly-created London Country Bus Services Ltd, a subsidiary of the National Bus Company. The GLC was relieved of its control over public transport in June 1984 with the establishment of London Regional Transport (LRT), directly answerable to the Department of Transport. At this stage London Transport operated a fleet of about 6,000 vehicles from over 60 garages, supported by a vast engineering and bureaucratic machine. Some attempt at devolving operations to a local level was made through the existence of six operating divisions, although these had relatively little autonomy. The legislation setting up LRT also made provision for it to award contracts to operate bus services to operators after a competitive tendering process and, in anticipation of this, the bus operations were transferred to an arm's-length company, London Buses Ltd, in March 1985. The first contract awarded to a private company to operate buses was won by Len Wright Travel in July 1985 which took over route 81 linking Slough and Hounslow. Other routes, mainly in the outer suburbs, were tendered and, in the early stages, London Buses, with its high cost base, did not fare too well. One consequence of this was the establishment of low-cost operations such

Although both London Central and London General are relatively new companies, their heritage dates back to the earliest days of British bus operation. Seen at London Bus Museum, Brooklands, are preserved Leyland X2 LN 7270, delivered to London Central in 1908, and London General K502 (XC 8059) built by AEC.

The mainstay of the London Central fleet at privatisation was the Leyland Titan. T1000 (ALM 1B), seen at Holborn in May 2002, was one of a small number of buses to gain an electronic destination display.

as Stanwell Buses (which traded as Westlink), Kingston Bus, Bexleybus and Suttonbus, which were able to bid for work at more competitive rates.

The intention was that London's bus services would ultimately be deregulated and privatised in the same way as elsewhere in the UK, and as a first step towards this, London Buses Ltd was reorganised from 1 January 1989 into 11 smaller units, each with its own operating licence. With the exception of Stanwell Buses, which had its own licence, the low-cost units were reincorporated into one of the new operations. A separate business, London Coaches, assumed control of the Round London Sightseeing Tour and a number of commuter operations linking the capital with north Kent.

In December 1992 the Minister of Transport in London, Steven Norris announced that privatisation of London's bus-operating companies would take place, with deregulation following by mid-1995.

Go-Ahead Northern very nearly became the first purchaser of a London bus-operating company as it had made an offer of £2.5 million for Stanwell Buses, keen to use it as a springboard for further growth in a deregulated environment. In November 1993, however, the government announced that deregulation would not take place and the bid was withdrawn. Stanwell Buses was sold to its management team on 19 January 1994.

Although a significant proportion of the network had been tendered by this stage, there still remained a large part that was operated by London Buses' subsidiaries under a block grant from LRT. In order to create a level playing field this arrangement was ended and individual five-year contracts were awarded for each route by the newly established London Transport Buses. The bulk of contracts were awarded on a net cost basis, where revenue was retained by the operator, rather than the gross cost basis previously preferred. It was felt that this would encourage operators to run services better as they carried the revenue risk.

On 24 March 1994 the government announced that it intended to complete the sale of London Buses' companies by the end of the year. Offers were invited from prospective purchasers by late May, with shortlisted bidders being announced in July. Although all London Buses' vehicles carried red livery, those provided by independent operators were in their own schemes. This had given rise to concerns that the privatisation process would lead to the end of London's iconic red bus and it was therefore stated that all future contracts awarded for services within central London must use buses that were 80% red.

The sales process was rapid with the first deal being completed by the end of August. On 23 September it was announced that Go-Ahead had been successful in its bid for London Central, which operated 498 buses from four garages, at Camberwell (which also housed its head office), Peckham, New Cross and Bexleyheath, where it had gained the contracts for the bulk of the former Bexleybus network. London Central was the fourth operation to be sold, although ratification of the £23.8 million deal had to wait until it was cleared by an extraordinary meeting of

The Routemaster featured in both London fleets, five routes using the type at privatisation. London Central applied route branding to the vehicles used on its two services, the 12 and 36. RML2273 is seen at Marble Arch operating on route 12X, an extra service run in connection with the Notting Hill carnival, in August 2004.

London General's standard double-deck bus at the time of its acquisition by Go-Ahead was the MCW Metrobus. M1357 (C357 BUV) shows off the London General livery to good effect as it passes along Great Smith Street, Westminster.

shareholders on 17 October. The London Central fleetname has its origins in the establishment of the London Central Omnibus Co in 1906. The company was supported by Leyland Motors whose products, not surprisingly, formed the bulk of its fleet. By 1913, when it was taken over by London General, the fleet had grown to about 100 vehicles.

The majority of the fleet in 1994 was made up of Leyland Titans (262), the youngest of which was 11 years old, and Routemasters (104), although there were also 24 nearly-new Optare Spectras together with 27 Dennis Darts. Other small-bus requirements were met largely by Optare StarRider and MetroRider minibuses. With the exception of the Routemasters, which were red with a white cantrail band, these vehicles were all in the then-standard London Buses livery of red with a grey skirt and thin white cantrail band. They carried London Central's fleetname and stylised "Thames Clipper" logo together with the London Buses roundel, which was removed quickly after the sale.

Early successes in the tendering market saw the fleet grow in size with Northern Counties-bodied Volvo Olympians the preferred choice, to both single- and dual-door layouts. A small number of Olympians with Alexander Royale bodywork were also acquired from dealer stock. The Routemaster fleet, used on routes 12 and 36, received distinctive route branding.

On 24 May 1996 Go-Ahead acquired London General for £46 million. London General had been the largest London Buses subsidiary when purchased in November 1994 by a management team led by Keith Ludeman for £32 million, with a fleet of over 600 buses operating from six garages in south London. Metrobuses and Routemasters dominated the double-deck fleet, although it had also received 39 Volvo Citybuses for use on routes 133 and 196. Its single-deck fleet was formed largely of Dennis Darts together with various minibuses and a fleet of 42 Leyland National Greenways, used on the Red Arrow services in central London. In May 1993 additional variety had been injected into the fleet with the arrival of 13 Northern Counties-bodied Volvo B10Bs for use on route 88, linking Oxford Circus with Clapham Common. The buses carried a revised iteration of London Buses' standard livery with a yellow "pencil line" separating the grey skirt from the red bodywork and were branded "The Clapham Omnibus". They also had select registrations featuring the initials of Keith Ludeman. The use of full-size single-decker buses was unusual on a central London route and was intended as an experiment to ascertain whether they presented operational problems.

The London General name dates back to 1855 when the Compagnie Générale des Omnibus de Londres, which traded as General, was formed to bring together many of the horse bus operations in the capital. As can be inferred from the company's name, there was a significant level of French backing to the new enterprise, although local opposition to foreign involvement saw the company name anglicised to London General Omnibus Company (LGOC) from 1859. The LGOC grew quickly, usually by acquiring the assets and operations of other operations once they had failed, and soon became the largest bus operator in London. It began using motor omnibuses in

London General used the "Streetline" brand for a number of minibus services. Optare MetroRider MRL223 (K223 MGT) is seen in 1995. (Haydn Davies)

Large numbers of Northern Counties-bodied Volvo Olympians joined the London fleets between 1995 and 1998. NV60 (260 CLT) is seen laying over at Lewisham during July 1998. Several buses in the London fleets have received cherished registrations from Routemasters over the years.

1902, with the last horse-drawn bus running in 1911. In 1912, the Underground Group, which owned most of the London Underground, bought the LGOC and its operations passed to the LPTB in 1933.

The newly privatised operation adopted a livery based upon that used on "The Clapham Omnibus" together with a fleetname which contained an image of a B-type bus from the early days of London's motor buses.

In 1996 London General was successful in retaining contracts for several routes in the Sutton area. New vehicles were ordered in the form of low-floor Plaxton-bodied Dennis Darts for single-deck requirements and Northern Counties-bodied Volvo Olympians for double-deck routes. Although delivery did not commence until after London General had passed to Go-Ahead, both types fitted in well with the London Central fleet and were numbered in a common sequence.

London Central and London General retained their separate identities but the opportunity to rationalise operations was taken and most accounting, administration and engineering functions were brought together under a single management based at the latter's Mitcham base, with Keith Ludeman heading the combined operation. The only external sign of change was the adoption of London General's livery style by the London Central fleet.

Go-Ahead's London fleets operated over 170 Routemasters. Whilst the 126 RMLs had been extensively refurbished and fitted with new Cummins or Iveco engines in the early 1990s, the shorter RMs, which formed a significant part of the allocation, were beginning to look tired. A programme was therefore initiated in 1997 to upgrade their interiors and fit more modern Scania engines, which improved both reliability and emissions levels. The year also saw the Volvo B10Bs used on route 88 replaced by Metrobuses from 29 March. The Volvos, having lost their select registrations, were transferred to City of Oxford. The London labour market during the late 1990s was very tight and most bus operators faced significant difficulties in recruiting and retaining drivers. South-west London was particularly affected and London General therefore set up recruitment campaigns in north-east, north-west and south-west England. The latter was particularly successful, although increases in pay rates also helped improve the situation. Go-Ahead's London operations have continued to invest heavily in staff training and development and a dedicated facility is maintained, based at Camberwell garage. The company was one of the first London bus operators to adopt the national BTEC qualifications established by Edexcel for both controllers and drivers, improving customer service and providing staff with a more fulfilling job, thus reducing turnover.

During the latter part of the 1990s large numbers of new buses joined the fleet, usually in connection with the successful retention or gaining of tender awards. Following the earlier practice adopted by both London Central and London General, deliveries were standardised on Plaxton-bodied Dennis Darts and Northern Counties-bodied

London Central was successful in winning the contract to operate services linking the Millennium Dome at North Greenwich with Greenwich and Charlton. DAF/East Lancs Myllennium MD7 is seen at North Greenwich station on 19 February 2000.

Volvo Olympians. Some variety was provided in 1997 when a batch of 27 Volvo Olympians was ordered with Northern Counties' restyled Palatine II bodywork for use on route 74. Unusually for a London bus, these vehicles also had coach-style high-backed seating.

In 1999 Keith Ludeman moved across to manage the Group's growing rail division. His successor as Managing Director for the London operations was David Brown, who had previously been Operations Director.

The opening of the Jubilee Line extension in 1999 and the Millennium Dome at the end of the year prompted a number of changes to bus services in much of south-east London. London Central was successful in winning the contract to provide two high-quality routes, branded "Millennium Transit" and numbered M1 and M2, connecting the Dome with Charlton and Greenwich stations respectively. Although it was originally intended that part of the route would employ an innovative contactless guidance system, technical problems precluded this. The buses were, however, distinctive, being the first examples of East Lancs' stylish Myllennium body built on a DAF chassis. Internally, they featured air conditioning and an audio-visual passenger information system whilst, externally, powered destination blinds ensured correctly set displays. Three of the 17 buses were powered by compressed natural gas. It had originally been intended to withdraw routes M1 and M2 after the millennium celebrations ended on 31 December 2000, but by this time the Jubilee Line station at North Greenwich had become a significant transport hub in its own right. As a result, from 23 February 2001 route M1 was incorporated into a new route, the 486, which was operated by London Central initially using the DAFs until contract renewal in 2007 saw them replaced by double-deckers.

Although low-floor single-deckers had become universal by 1997, the first such double-deckers did not enter service in the capital until late 1998. Go-Ahead London's first examples, a batch of 46 Alexander ALX400-bodied Volvo B7TLs, entered service with London Central on 28 January 2000. Further examples of the Volvo chassis, with Plaxton President bodywork, became the standard double-decker for most deliveries until 2005, with over 400 joining the fleet. Some variety was provided for in the shape of 52 Volvo B7TLs with East Lancs Vyking bodywork delivered to London General in 2002 and 50 Dennis Tridents with Plaxton bodywork delivered in two batches in 2000 and 2002/3.

The Labour government elected in May 1997 had pledged to reintroduce a London-wide authority which would include transport as one of its responsibilities. In anticipation of this there was a change to the tendering system which saw a return to gross cost contracts from August 1998 whilst details of a new system were developed. On 1 April 2000 LTB became London Bus Services Ltd (LBSL). The new organisation was part of Transport for London (TfL), which fell under the control of the newly created Greater London Authority (GLA) upon its inception on 3 July 2000.

The GLA, under Mayor Ken Livingstone, saw increased bus use as the key to addressing London's transport problems, and bus fares were generally capped with new categories of Travelcards and saver tickets giving

Over 400 Volvo B7TLs with Plaxton President bodywork entered service between 2000 and 2005. Although most remain in service on TfL routes, some have been cascaded to provincial fleets whilst others, including London General PVL263 (PN02 XBL), have joined the Commercial Services fleet.

further discounts. The tendering system was revised and from October 2000 Quality Incentive Contracts (QIC) were introduced in which TfL retains revenue but with incentive provisions in the form of performance-related payment bonuses and deductions for the operator if certain criteria are not met. Although initially awarded for five years, an option to extend the contract by a further two years is available if operators meet their targets.

By the summer of 2001 passenger numbers on London bus services were growing strongly. This prompted TfL to increase frequencies and convert a number of single-deck operations to double-deckers. The effect of these initiatives was dramatic. At the time of privatisation the combined fleet size of the London Central and London Central fleets was just over 1100 vehicles, a figure that had barely changed by 1999. In the following ten years it grew to the extent that by 2010 the fleets operated over 1500 buses.

In 2002 contracts to operate the Red Arrow services, a network with heavy peak loadings that effectively fills gaps in the Underground network, were re-awarded to London General with articulated buses replacing the Leyland National Greenways then in use. This represented the first regular use of artics on the London bus network and a system of open boarding, in which passengers had to purchase tickets before travel, was adopted to speed up journeys. A fleet of 31 Mercedes-Benz Citaro G buses took over operation on 6 June 2002. The year also saw the first Volvo B7TLs to carry Wrightbus's distinctive Eclipse Gemini bodywork join the fleet. The influx of new vehicles helped lead to the withdrawal of the last Metrobuses in February 2003 whilst the last Leyland Titan operated in service on 19 June of that year.

A key component of the Mayor's transport strategy was the introduction of congestion charging in the central area from February 2003, with the revenue raised funding major improvements to bus services. This saw a number of routes being split into overlapping sections which provided more buses over the common section of route. One of the more significant developments of this type saw the introduction of route 436 to parallel a part of route 36, operated by London Central with Routemasters from New Cross garage. The new route, introduced on 8 February 2003, was operated by 30 artics and marked the beginning of a plan to convert the capital's busiest routes to this mode of operation.

The introduction of route 436 saw a reduction in the peak vehicle requirement on route 36 from 47 to 26 Routemasters. Although a five-year QIC had been re-awarded to London General in November 2002 for Routemaster operation of route 14, it was clear that TfL now intended to remove them from frontline service. There were a number of reasons for this apparent change of direction. Not only were the vehicles becoming

On 5 June 2002 London General became the first operator of articulated buses in normal London service when routes 507 and 521 were converted to this mode of operation. MAL31 (BX02 YZT) is seen crossing London Bridge. Although 12 of London's busiest routes received artics, a change in Mayoral policy saw them withdrawn by 2012.

Since 2006 double-deck deliveries have included ADL's Enviro400, which were the first vehicles in the fleet to meet Euro IV emission standards. London Central E55 (LX56 EUC) approaches North Greenwich station when new.

increasingly elderly but the spread of off-bus ticketing, a process given added momentum with the introduction of Oyster in 2003, had rendered the traditional conductor's role largely redundant. In addition, the increasingly litigious nature of society had led to an upsurge in claims from passengers alleging that they had fallen from open platforms. Finally, and crucially, Routemasters did not meet modern accessibility requirements. The replacement of Routemasters began in earnest on 1 November 2003 when London General's route 11 lost its RMLs in favour of new low-floor double-deckers. The next Routemaster conversion to affect a Go-Ahead London route saw London Central's 12 converted on 5 November, commencing a new contract ushering in Mercedes-Benz Citaro articulated buses. London Central's last Routemasters ran on route 36 after service on 28 January 2005, the route gaining some of the last Plaxton President-bodied Volvo B7TLs to be built. The contract for the 36, which ran until 27 May 2007, was modified to reflect the change of vehicle type and mode.

A contract amendment from 23 July 2005 heralded the end of Routemasters on Putney garage's routes 14 and 22. It is noteworthy that one of the Routemasters withdrawn, RML2590, had spent its entire working life at this garage, having been allocated there when new in November 1966. This conversion saw the end of regular operation of Routemasters, or for that matter any half-cab buses, by the Go-Ahead Group.

Although the withdrawal of Routemasters attracted a lot of interest in both the enthusiast and general press, most of it hostile, it was part of a wider initiative to make London's bus fleet wholly low-floor by the end of 2005, an objective which was met. A consequence of this was the cascade of a number of relatively new buses from the Group's London fleets to regional operations.

The nature of the London tendering process means that approximately 20% of the network is tendered each year and, inevitably, some of it changes hands. Although bids are always submitted with a view to retaining existing work, there is always the unknown quantity of the nature of other bidders and work can be lost. In 2004/5 both companies lost over 60 buses' worth of work to other operators. This was more than compensated in April 2006 when London Central took over routes 68, 468 and X68 from Arriva London South, representing over 70 vehicles. To meet this requirement further Wright-bodied Volvo B7TLs were ordered. These buses, which were the last of the type for Go-Ahead's London fleets, featured a revised destination display in which a single-line destination, alongside the route number, replaced the traditional use of "via" points on London buses. The change, to meet TfL requirements, became standard for all future orders. A further, subtle, change in TfL's requirements saw all new buses and repaints from late 2005 have a white roof, to help keep buses cool in summer.

Environmental considerations have led to increasing emphasis being placed on reducing vehicle emissions, particularly in urban areas. In 2003 it was announced that London Central's route 360 would act as a testing

London Central was the first operator in the UK to use hybrid buses in regular service when six Wright Electrocitys (later joined by a seventh) were delivered for TfL route 360 in 2005. London's initial hybrids carried a distinctive livery promoting their green credentials. Further similar buses arrived during 2011 to allow the whole route to be converted to this mode of operation.

In September 2006 London General acquired Docklands Buses, based in Silvertown. The following summer further expansion in east London saw the bus operations of Blue Triangle join the fleet. The latter's traditionally-styled livery is seen on TL905B (V905 FEC), an East Lancs Lolyne-bodied Dennis Trident. This bus had been rebodied in 2003 after an arson attack.

ground for hybrid vehicles. Although it was originally intended to use Transbus Enviro200H hybrids, the collapse of Transbus into administration prevented this and the order was instead placed with Wrightbus for its Electrocity, with the first vehicles delivered in the spring of 2006. They carried prominent branding advertising their green credentials, together with a leaf pattern over their red bodysides. During the summer of 2011 further similar buses joined the fleet, thus making route 360 the first operated by Go-Ahead London scheduled for 100% operation by hybrid buses. The earlier buses were modified to match the newer vehicles.

In April 2006 David Brown took up a rôle as Managing Director of London's Surface Transport for TfL. His successor was John Trayner, who had joined the Group in 2002 as Operations Director, having previously held senior positions at Arriva London.

In May 2006 London General placed the first Alexander Dennis (ADL) Enviro400 buses to be equipped with Euro IV engines into service on route 196. These use a selective catalytic reduction process to reduce emissions whilst their lightweight construction helps save fuel and, therefore, reduce emissions still further. Further similar vehicles joined both fleets as TfL's vehicle noise limits had effectively prevented further orders being placed for Volvo's B7TL chassis.

On 18 September 2006 Go-Ahead announced that, through London General, it had acquired Docklands Minibuses Ltd. This represented Go-Ahead's entry into the East London bus market, seen as being an area with significant growth potential both in the run-up to the 2012 Olympics and thereafter as a result of the regeneration of that part of London being actively pursued by the government.

The company had its antecedents in Docklands Transit, a subsidiary of Transit Holdings, run by Harry Blundred. The operation of buses outside of the London tendering system did not prove viable and the company bid for a number of tendered services. In July 1997 Docklands Transit was purchased by Stagecoach and its operations integrated with those of East London, whilst Docklands Minibuses Ltd retained its residual private-hire business. In March 2002 this company gained its first TfL contract, for route 167 using a fleet of Caetano-bodied Dennis Darts carrying "Docklands Buses" fleetnames. Other contract successes followed, and at the time of the takeover some 30 vehicles were in use on four routes. Initially, vehicles used on TfL contracts carried pale blue and white relief, although all-over red was later adopted.

Further expansion in east London took place in June 2007 with the purchase of Rainham-based Blue Triangle Buses' London tendered operations for £12 million. Blue Triangle had been established by Roger Wright in October 1985 and was perhaps best known for its heritage fleet of London buses, which were not acquired, and continue to trade as The London Bus Company. It operated a fleet of approximately 60 vehicles on eight TfL contracts and nine contracts for Essex County Council. Although more recent arrivals had been painted all-over red, its livery had previously been a rather traditional red and cream.

The successful retention of the Sutton-area routes in December 2008 saw a large number of new vehicles arrive at Merton and Sutton garages. Optare bodywork was fitted to 40 ADL Enviro200 single-deckers and 54 Trident double-deckers. SOE8 (LX09 AYN) shows the revised fleetname style adopted for the London fleets from 2006.

Expansion in east London saw Blue Triangle awarded the contract to operate routes EL1 and EL2, branded East London Transit, which commenced on 20 February 2010. The services, which benefit from high-quality roadside infrastructure and bus priority measures, are provided by 16 Volvo B9TLs with Wright Eclipse Gemini 2 bodywork.

The first ADL Enviro200Darts, an updated version of the well-established type, joined the London General fleet in March 2007 with further orders following. In August 2008 the Docklands Buses operation received nine Scania OmniCity double-deckers, the first for Go-Ahead's London fleet. These vehicles introduced a new style of fleetname which saw the Go-Ahead London brand used for the first time accompanied by a strapline carrying the operator's name. Later in the year three Volvo B9TLs with Alexander Dennis Enviro400 bodywork joined the London General fleet. With the exception of a demonstrator provided by Volvo in 2006, these were the first new Volvo buses for use on TfL services for over two years.

In February 2008 London General won the tender to operate route 453 previously run by Selkent. This was the first, and as subsequent events proved, only, service operated by articulated buses to change operators and retain this mode of operation at re-tendering. A further 25 Mercedes artics, to Euro V specification, joined the fleet, with a slightly modified front and rear design compared to previous vehicles.

The Sutton area network was re-tendered from December 2008. In order to meet the requirement for new vehicles a batch of 54 Optare Olympus-bodied ADL Tridents and 40 Optare Esteem-bodied ADL Darts were ordered. Both combinations are unique in the Go-Ahead London fleets, with the latter representing the last of the Esteem body style produced.

In the summer of 2008 TfL announced that it was to part-fund the provision of 43 hybrid buses for service in London. Of this figure five ADL Enviro400H double-deckers and a solitary Wrightbus hybrid were delivered to London General's Stockwell garage in early 2009 for use on route 24, although whilst crew training was under way they operated on route 196 as this passed the garage. A diesel-engined Wrightbus integral was also acquired and allocated initially to Camberwell garage for use on routes 68/468 and X68, although it later transferred to Stockwell.

Although many TfL tender awards are still made on the basis of new vehicles, there has been an increasing trend in recent years to specify either existing buses or a mix of new and existing vehicles which clearly helps reduce costs. The existing vehicles are, however, subjected to a major refurbishment which in effect returns them to "as new" condition.

As has been well documented elsewhere, the operation of "bendy buses" in the capital has been controversial ever since they were launched, with critics arguing that they are unsuited to London's street layout and that the open-boarding approach encouraged fare evasion. Their replacement became a central plank of Boris Johnson's successful Mayoral campaign in 2008 and he pledged that they would be withdrawn. It was, in many respects, unfortunate that the first routes operated by such vehicles to fall due for re-tendering were the Red Arrow services, on which they were most suitable. London General bid successfully to operate both routes with a fleet of new rigid Mercedes-Benz Citaros which took over route 507 from 25 July 2009 and 521 from 1 September. A late-evening service was introduced on both routes, the 507 also gaining a weekend service. The lower passenger capacity of the new vehicles meant that a fleet of 49 was required to replace the artics. The new buses also saw the discontinuation of the "Red Arrow" brand originally adopted by London Transport in 1966 to identify its central London limited-stop flat-fare services.

In July 2009 the withdrawal of London articulated buses commenced with the replacement of those used on Red Arrow route 507 with rigid Mercedes-Benz Citaros. MEC4 (BG09 JJV) passes the Palace of Westminster on its first day in service.

Buses used on TfL contracts now carry all-over red livery with a "Buses" roundel. Volvo B5LH/Wrightbus WHV1 (LJ61 GVW), seen crossing Westminster Bridge, is one of a growing number of hybrid buses in the Go-Ahead London fleet.

In the summer of 2008 TfL announced that it would investigate the potential for private-sector involvement in running its East Thames Buses (ETB) subsidiary. ETB had been established in 2000 after east London operator Harris Bus went into administration. Attempts to find other operators prepared to take on the contracts failed and it was recognised that the only immediate option was to set up an in-house operation. The company came to be seen as the operator of last resort, available to step in if another provider failed, if tender prices were unacceptably high or performance particularly poor. Thus it operated routes 42 and 185, which had been taken over following the collapse of London Easylink and the 201, assumed when Mitcham Belle ceased running buses for TfL. Its portfolio also included what is probably London's most challenging bus route, the 108, which runs through the Blackwall Tunnel where endemic traffic congestion hampers reliable operation. Uniquely, ETB did not bid for routes through the tendering process – it was allocated them by TfL in order to give it a balanced portfolio of work and minimise dead mileage. On 30 July 2009 it was announced that agreement had been reached for ETB to be acquired by the Go-Ahead Group for £5 million and that it would pass to London General on 5 September. As part of the deal London General was awarded five-year QICs in respect of ETB's routes and quickly initiated a programme to refurbish and repaint the fleet. Although ETB had been sold to London General, the opportunity was taken to reallocate routes to London Central where this was more efficient from an operational standpoint.

Towards the end of 2009 the first of a large order of Volvo B9TL buses with Wright Eclipse Gemini 2 bodywork started to arrive for contract renewals on routes 45 and 63. A further batch of 16 similar vehicles was delivered to Blue Triangle for the launch, on 20 February 2010, of East London Transit routes EL1 and EL2. The new network, which includes high-quality roadside infrastructure and bus priority measures, supports the regeneration of the Barking and Dagenham Dock areas where a large amount of new housing is being built. The buses carry a distinctive livery of red and orange with bold branding. Further tender renewals saw double-deck orders split between ADL's Enviro400 and the Wrightbus-bodied Volvo B9TL.

The potential for growth in east London was amply demonstrated in September 2011 when Blue Triangle and Docklands Buses won TfL contracts for six routes requiring over 60 vehicles, practically doubling the size of the Docklands Buses fleet. During the autumn of 2011 TfL's policy to withdraw articulated buses from London saw routes 12, 436 and 453, with a combined peak vehicle requirement of over 100 vehicles, receive diesel-powered Enviro400s and Volvo B9TLs together with Enviro400H and Volvo B5LH hybrid buses. These vehicles carried a simpler all-over red livery mandated by TfL which included the organisation's new "Buses" roundel, modelled on the famous London Transport "bullseye", which had begun to appear on new and repainted buses from the summer of 2011. Expansion has continued into 2012 with contract gains and the acquisition, in March, of the Northumberland Park operations of First London East.

Although Go-Ahead London is primarily an operator of local bus services under contract to TfL, it also maintains a significant commercial services fleet which provides special services for a number of events in London and the Home Counties. In addition it runs a number of services under contract to both Essex and Surrey county councils and is a major provider of buses for rail-replacement operations, particularly for fellow Go-Ahead operators South Eastern and Southern. Its fleet includes open-toppers and a small number of Routemasters which are popular for private-hire duties. It also has been awarded the contract to transport all Olympics officials for the 2012 games and to run one of the three Olympic transport depots being established by the London Organising Committee of the Olympic Games.

Go-Ahead London provides over 16% of the London bus market, and accounts for approximately 365 million bus journeys annually on nearly 100 day and night routes. It is, by some margin, the largest bus operation in the Group by turnover and carries more passengers than the other bus-operating companies combined. Although the economic climate over the next few years will be challenging, with TfL putting pressure on operators' margins, Go-Ahead London is well placed to increase its profile in the London bus market and will work with TfL to help deliver the Mayor's vision for transport in the capital.

Chapter 7

Rail Franchising
An improving journey

By 1992, when a Conservative government was re-elected, the vast majority of bus operation in mainland Britain was in the hands of the private sector and plans were well advanced to sell off London Buses' subsidiary companies. A key manifesto commitment of the Conservative Party had been the privatisation of British Rail (BR), which proved to be the last major divestment of State assets undertaken by the 1979-97 Conservative government and was, in the event, completed only weeks before the Labour Party, led by Tony Blair, gained power.

Although a number of options were considered, including selling BR as a single concern and splitting it into regional companies (similar to the pre-nationalisation "Big Four"), the chosen approach was to create a separate authority, Railtrack, to own and maintain the track and other fixed infrastructure with other, often competing, companies established to deliver the operational side of running the railway. Railtrack was to be sold by means of a Stock Market flotation. It was decided that passenger rail services would be provided by private-sector Train Operating Companies (TOCs) which would compete for franchises to operate trains for a specified period. In advance of this process, BR established 25 train operating units (TOUs) in early 1994, which operated as "shadow franchises" in order to provide financial and other information needed by potential franchisees.

It was recognised that although franchises were to be awarded from periods of seven to 15 years, the lifespan of railway rolling stock was considerably longer than this. As such it would have been unlikely that franchisees would take on the long-term financial commitments associated with procuring trains themselves, so ownership of BR's passenger rolling stock therefore passed to three leasing companies established for the purpose.

The process of overseeing the franchising process, and ensuring that the level and quality of service was maintained, was initially given to the Office of Passenger Rail Franchising (OPRAF). Its functions passed to the

Initially a joint venture with its management, Go-Ahead operated the Thames Trains franchise from September 1996 until March 2004. Its modern fleet consisted entirely of Turbo diesel multiple-units, of which 165116 is seen approaching Reading with a service from London Paddington. (Tony Miles)

The Thameslink franchise was awarded to Govia, a joint venture between Go-Ahead and VIA-GTI (later renamed Keolis). It operated services across London such as this Bedford–Brighton train seen passing South Croydon in August 2005.

newly established Strategic Rail Authority in 2001 although, following the SRA's abolition in 2006, responsibility passed to the Department for Transport.

To ensure the efficient operation of the rail industry, in the interests of consumers, operators and government, the statutory office of Rail Regulator was established. The office was abolished from July 2004, with its functions taken over by a nine-member board called the Office of Rail Regulation.

A serious rail crash at Hatfield in the autumn of 2000 exposed major failings in Railtrack's maintenance procedures. The costs incurred in rectifying this rendered the company insolvent and it was placed into administration on 7 October 2001. Just under 12 months later, the administration order was discharged and a new not-for-profit company, Network Rail, took control of the rail infrastructure.

The rail franchising process started in May 1995 when invitations to tender were issued to prospective operators. In the early stages, there was considerable uncertainty as to how much serious interest there would be in the process, especially as the Labour Party was threatening to return the rail network to public ownership if it won the general election due no later than May 1997.

The opportunity to expand into the rail market attracted the Group and it was actively involved in submitting bids to run five franchises in the initial tendering rounds. Only one of these, an unsuccessful attempt to secure the contract to operate Merseyrail Electrics, was submitted in its own right. The remaining bids were made either jointly with management or through Govia, a joint venture between the Go-Ahead Group and VIA-GTI, a French-owned transport provider. In 1999 SNCF acquired a majority stake in VIA-GTI and merged it with its Carianne subsidiary, branding the enlarged operation VIA-Carianne. A change of name to Keolis took place in 2001.

Train operating companies in which the Group had a significant involvement were successful in winning two of the first rail franchises to be awarded.

Thames Trains operated the Thames Valley commuter trains from Paddington as well as longer-distance services to Stratford-upon-Avon and Hereford, and the cross-country link between Gatwick Airport and Reading using a fleet of relatively modern Class 165 and 166 "Thames Turbo" diesel multiple-units (DMUs). The franchise was awarded to Victory Railway Holdings Ltd, a joint venture between the Go-Ahead Group and Thames Trains management in which the Group held a 65% share. Operations commenced in September 1996 with the contract set to end on 31 March 2004. In June 1998 the Group acquired the shares held by Thames Trains' management team and henceforth ran the franchise in its own right.

Govia took over the South Central franchise from Connex in August 2001. Showing the new livery adopted is Class 421 EMU 1738, seen at Clapham Junction next to a train still carrying Connex livery. A key franchise commitment was the withdrawal of slam-door rolling stock by the end of 2005. (Tony Miles)

The Southern network includes only two non-electrified lines: those from Oxted to Uckfield and between Ashford and Hastings. Seen at Edenbridge Town forming a service from London Bridge to Uckfield is 171804, one of 15 Turbostar trains built by Bombardier and operated by Southern. The "Southern" brand, adopted from May 2004, is clearly seen on the station sign.

The relatively short length of the franchise, and the comparative youth of the rolling stock, meant that there was no requirement to procure new trains; however, in the autumn of 2000 Thames Trains commenced the refurbishment of the Class 166 DMUs used on longer-distance services. The work included replacement of the air-conditioning system and upgraded interior fittings. The units received a new Thames Trains Express livery, befitting the type of routes on which they were operated.

On 5 October 1999 a Thames Trains service from Paddington to Bedwyn passed through a red signal and collided with the 06:03 First Great Western service from Cheltenham to London. A total of 31 people, including the drivers of both trains, were killed and over 200 required hospital treatment for their injuries. The accident highlighted significant shortcomings in both driver training – the driver of the Thames Trains service had only recently qualified – and emergency evacuation procedures on trains. Thames Trains was subsequently fined £2 million for breaches of health and safety law and a wide-reaching reappraisal of training programmes was undertaken across the industry, together with upgraded passenger safety information in trains.

Following a review of rail franchises the Strategic Rail Authority announced its intention to reduce the number of franchises, with the specific aim of having one operator per London terminal station. This resulted in the Thames Trains franchise being subsumed into that for other services from Paddington operated by First Great Western when the initial contract expired in April 2004 pending the award of a new franchise. This also incorporated the former Wessex Trains franchise running regional services in the south-west of England.

Govia was successful in winning the franchise to operate Thameslink, the north-south rail service through the heart of London, for seven years and a day from 2 March 1997. Thameslink provided two distinct operations: long-distance services linking Bedford with Brighton, and a suburban service linking Luton with Sutton and Wimbledon. Its fleet of Class 319 electric multiple-units used two distinct brands – City Flier covered long services from the south coast to Bedford whilst inner-suburban trains operated as City Metro – although all trains carried the same dark blue and yellow livery. The City Flier fleet was refurbished during the late 1990s with improved interior décor and increased luggage space for the benefit of passengers travelling to London Gatwick Airport. Thameslink also ran close to Luton Airport, served by a dedicated bus service from Luton Airport Parkway station which opened in 1999.

Govia's franchise was extended for two years; however, when it expired in April 2006 the Thameslink services were incorporated within a new franchise, which included Great Northern suburban services from King's Cross which was awarded to FirstGroup.

In 1999 Govia, in conjunction with Swedish operator BK-Tåg, was successful in bidding to provide both the Stockholm commuter network and inter-city services linking Gothenburg and Malmo. Unforeseen difficulties meant, however, that Go-Ahead withdrew its involvement from this operation.

Most medium- and longer-distance trains on the Southern network are formed of Electrostar EMUs, in three- and four-car formations. One of the latter, 377106, is seen approaching Ford on the Coastway line.

Southern (formerly South Central)

In October 2000 it was announced that Govia, through its New Southern Railway subsidiary, had been made the preferred bidder for the South Central franchise to operate trains between London and the south coast in place of Connex. This was the first time that a rail franchise had passed from one private operator to another, and in order to smooth the transition both parties agreed to the change of operator taking place from 26 August 2001, some two years before the expiry date of the original franchise. The original expectation was that a new franchise starting in May 2003 would have been offered for 20 years; however, the SRA ultimately decided on cost grounds to award it for seven years. Although this clearly limited the scope for long-term investment, Govia committed itself to replacing the large fleet of slam-door trains by the end of 2005 and working with Network Rail to eliminate pinch points in order to improve reliability. In addition, there was significant investment in upgrading station depot facilities.

September 2003 saw the introduction, in conjunction with South West Trains and South Eastern, of the "Overground Network" covering suburban lines in south London. Designed to encourage off-peak travel by providing consistent frequency (at least four trains per hour), improved passenger information and security, the initiative was funded jointly by TfL, the SRA and operators.

In its early days the franchise traded as South Central, although its new livery became an increasingly common sight as trains were repainted, losing the somewhat insipid Connex yellow and white scheme. On 30 May 2004 the new operation was formally launched as "Southern", re-creating the heyday of the pre-nationalisation Southern Railway. The new brand, which was quickly applied to trains, stations and staff uniforms, was only part of the picture as Southern had to regain the confidence of passengers, which had taken a severe knock under Connex management.

During the first term of Southern's franchise, over £1 billion was invested in the biggest upgrade to the network since electrification in the 1930s. Frontline staff benefited from an improved working environment as well as opportunities for training and development, whilst managers were expected to undergo an intensive leadership programme designed to reinforce the message that real change had to be driven from the top of the organisation. These initiatives were crucial in helping to address the poor labour relations that had pertained under Connex.

In addition to investing in a new fleet of Electrostars to replace slam-door electric multiple-units (EMUs), the ageing diesel-electric multiple-units used on services to Uckfield and between Hastings and Ashford were replaced by new Turbostar trains. Govia's original bid, based on a 20-year franchise, had envisaged electrifying these routes, but the business case did not stack up over a shorter franchise period so the plan was not taken forward. Southern did, however, commit to introducing more frequent services and extending the Ashford-to-Hastings services to Brighton. The existing inner-suburban fleet of Class 455 trains benefited from a £20 million refurbishment.

The high levels of peak demand experienced by commuter railways have always led to a certain amount of overcrowding. Southern employed a passenger load determination system in order to assess the extent of this. Analysis of the results showed that by applying a few minor alterations to train lengths it was possible to reduce overcrowding from 12% to about 3%. Further initiatives to manage demand more effectively included the adoption of an imaginative fares policy which used yield management to encourage passengers to use shoulder and off-peak services.

Since privatisation passenger numbers on Britain's railways have grown dramatically, causing capacity problems in some areas. In a bid to address these, Network Rail has undertaken a number of route utilisation studies, designed to allow optimum use of the rail infrastructure. One such review, published in April 2007, proposed incorporating the Gatwick Express franchise into that for South Central. Gatwick Express, launched in May 1984, was the first

The Gatwick Express franchise passed to Southern in June 2008. Services are now fully integrated with London–Brighton trains with 24 "Wessex Electric" trains, built in the 1980s for the Bournemouth line, providing inter-city levels of comfort.

Southeastern provides services between London and Kent. A fleet of Electrostars, such as 375615 seen at Waterloo East, is used on longer routes.

dedicated airport express rail service in the world and had been franchised to National Express for 15 years in 1996. It passed to Southern on 22 June 2008, along with some 300 staff. The introduction of refurbished Class 442 EMUs brought inter-city standards of comfort to the route and allowed the creation of a premium sub-brand for the Brighton, Gatwick Airport and Victoria corridor.

Govia was successful in retaining the franchise for Southern from 20 September 2009. The new franchise which, assuming a two-year extension is granted, runs until July 2017, will require a premium payment of £534 million in present value terms, by the end of the period. Significant levels of investment will be maintained and it is anticipated that by December 2013 capacity will have increased by 10% across the network.

In addition, over £70 million will be invested in improving trains and stations, targeting those areas of greatest benefit to passengers. This will see staffing at almost all Greater London stations extended to provide cover from the first to the last service, together with improved passenger access and integration at stations, making it easier to use the Southern network. The introduction of new ticket machines, together with Smartmedia, which makes ticket buying easier and enables automatic top-ups for season tickets at key stations, are supported by an improved revenue-protection regime which sees automatic ticket barriers installed, supported by a team of 100 Revenue Protection Officers.

Southern carries over 160 million passengers per year. Although the mainstay of its passenger base remains the London commuter market, it has developed innovative methods to attract customers to off-peak services in order to fill unused capacity. These include the use of online marketing and passenger databases to allow targeted offers. Although the main focus of Southern's operations is its services to London, it also provides trains on some relatively rural stretches of lines. Southern is a member of the Sussex Community Rail Partnership which aims to bring together train operators, Network Rail, local authorities and local communities to encourage the use of local railways and work together to improve their facilities.

In February 2012 Southern was named the Interfleet Technology Rail Business of the Year at the 2011 Rail Business Awards. In making the award, particular emphasis was placed on the "Eyewitness" scheme, an industry first that has seen every member of onboard staff, most station staff and all of the Safer Travel Team equipped with a BlackBerry so that they can instantly report any incidents or suspicious behaviour to more than 160 recipients. A pilot group of passengers are also able to use their own smartphones for the same purpose.

"Eyewitness" has enabled Southern to quickly identify trends in crime and disorder, crime hotspots and persistent offenders, helping in the development of long-term safety and security strategies. The results speak for themselves, with detection of antisocial behaviour raised 37% and detection of staff assaults increasing more than 17%.

In addition, Southern's environmental innovations, including the generation of its own electricity from solar panels and regenerative braking, as well as reducing electricity consumption by such means as intelligent lighting, were recognised.

The Southern network continues to see passenger growth and in December 2011 it announced an order for 130 new Electrostar carriages which will see most eight-coach trains lengthened to 10 coaches from December. In addition it has acquired 19 BR-era Class 313 EMUs which have been refurbished for use on Coastway services, thus releasing Electrostars for use elsewhere.

As part of its review of rail franchises, the Department for Transport (DfT) has decided that the Thameslink franchise will subsume Southern's operations from 2015. Govia has been shortlisted for the new Thameslink franchise, which will commence operating in the autumn of 2013. Although this process brings uncertainly to the Southern network, Govia remains committed to delivering further improvements for passengers during the current franchise, which runs until 2015. Success in the Thameslink franchise will allow it to deliver passenger benefits across the combined Thameslink and Southern networks.

Southeastern

The franchise to operate services on routes linking London with Kent and parts of East Sussex had been awarded to Connex for 15 years in 1996. It was subsequently amended to run until January 2007 when it would be incorporated into a new Integrated Kent Franchise to coincide with the start of domestic high-speed services. During 2003 the operator approached the DfT, stating that it would require an additional £58 million in subsidy to meet its contractual provisions. Rather than accede to the request for additional funding, the DfT gave notice that the franchise would cease no later than 21 December 2003. The short period of notice did not allow for a competition to identify a new franchisee and as a result operations were transferred to South Eastern Trains, a wholly-owned subsidiary of the SRA, from 8 November 2003.

It was always the intention that the South Eastern franchise would be re-tendered as soon as practicable and Govia was awarded an eight-year contract from 1 April 2006 with the option of a two-year extension subject to performance. The length of the franchise was largely determined by a desire to align it with the award of a new franchise to operate Thameslink following completion of upgrades to that line, currently due in December 2015. The cost profile anticipates a subsidy of £141 million in 2006/7, being replaced by a premium of £12.6 million in 2013/14.

The franchise complemented Govia's existing Southern franchise and reinforced its position as the pre-eminent operator of commuter rail services in the south-east. Although the bid had been made in the name of London & South Eastern Railway, it was decided to retain the Southeastern title, in recognition of the significant improvement in the reputation of the brand that had occurred whilst it was managed by the SRA.

Southeastern employs over 3,900 people and carries 157 million passengers per annum in one of the fastest-growing areas of the United Kingdom. At the start of the franchise its fleet consisted of both British Rail-era Networker EMUs, used on Metro services, and more recent Electrostars employed on longer-distance services.

As at Southern, staff had been through an unsettling period which Govia sought to address by investing in training and development. It quickly gained Investors in People (IiP) accreditation and has helped support over 35% of staff to gain a level 2 NVQ in customer service.

A significant boost to capacity occurred from 14 December 2009 when the Prime Minister, Gordon Brown, launched the UK's first domestic high-speed services, linking St Pancras with a number of destinations in Kent. The new services, provided by a fleet of 29 EMUs built by Hitachi, dramatically reduced journey times, with that from Ashford to London being cut from 83 minutes to just 37. In addition to making commuter journeys between

Jewel in the Southeastern crown is the high-speed service from St Pancras International. A pair of Hitachi-built Javelin trains are seen about to pass on the Medway viaduct. (Go-Ahead Group plc)

Southeastern operates nearly 200 Networker EMUs, built between 1991 and 1994 for use on suburban services. These units have recently undergone a refurbishment, and 465033 displays Southeastern's latest livery as it passes through Wandsworth Road.

London Midland has adopted a grey and black livery with green highlights. It is shown to good effect on 350125, one of 37 Siemens-built Desiro units introduced from October 2008.

east Kent and London a practicable proposition, the new services have also helped encourage off-peak day trips to destinations such as Canterbury, now only an hour from London. In May 2011 an extension to the high-speed network saw additional services launched linking Maidstone with London, with services to Sandwich and Deal following in September. The latter are crucial to helping the economic regeneration of the former Kent coalfield.

The high-speed trains also represented an integral part of the planning for the 2012 London Olympic Games with the "Olympic Javelin" transporting spectators from both central London and a park-and-ride site at Ebbsfleet to the Olympic venue in Stratford. In recognition of this the trains have been named after Britain's top athletes, including Dame Kelly Holmes and Sir Steve Redgrave.

Although clearly important, the high-speed services represent only 12% of Southeastern's capacity. The classic network is not being overlooked and a package of improvements to both trains and stations is being undertaken. The launch of high-speed services in December 2009 was accompanied by a fundamental recast of timetables on the remainder of the network, which capitalised on the increased capacity available. During the harsh winters of 2009 and 2010, Southeastern attracted criticism for the way in which it handled disruption caused by bad weather. A combination of geography, which means that the far south-east of England can experience heavy falls of relatively wet snow, and icing of the conductor rail, means that the railways of Kent are particularly vulnerable in such conditions. It is recognised that what customers expect most in such situations is reliable information. Southeastern has therefore worked with Network Rail to address the shortcomings and investment has been made to ensure that frontline staff can give accurate information to passengers as well as providing regular updates on the company's website.

Franchise agreements are highly specified by the DfT and generally based upon passenger and revenue assumptions derived from economic forecasts made at the time of the franchise bid. It is recognised that this arrangement gives limited flexibility for operators to respond to changing market circumstances. To mitigate this risk, the Southeastern franchise included a revenue share and support mechanism in which there was provision for DfT to share any revenue shortfall or benefit from income growth above the original projections from the fourth year of the franchise. As is widely known, the UK economy entered a lengthy recession towards the end of 2008, which severely impacted upon levels of new development, employment growth and passenger numbers. As a result Southeastern's revenue fell short of its target and it began to receive revenue support from April 2010.

Following a review of rail franchising undertaken by the coalition government elected in May 2010 it was announced that, in future, most rail franchises would be let for longer periods of up to 15 years. This change is designed to develop an environment in which franchises can invest in long-term improvements such as new trains and better stations. In addition, franchisees will be given greater freedom, within an overarching set of performance standards, to develop the business. The Southeastern franchise will not, however, be brought within the revised regime until after completion of Thameslink works at London Bridge, since this would adversely affect performance.

In March 2011 the DfT announced that, as Southeastern had met its performance targets, the option of extending its franchise to March 2014 was to be exercised.

London Midland

The 2004 review of rail franchising proposed the creation of a West Midlands franchise to combine the Silverlink County services from Euston with those of Central Trains operating in the West Midlands conurbation together with services from Birmingham to Liverpool. Both franchisees were part of the National Express Group.

In June 2007 it was announced that the new franchise had been awarded to Govia and would run from 11 November 2007 until 19 September 2015. The new operation adopted the "London Midland" brand, with echoes of the London Midland & Scottish Railway, and was based in Birmingham, recognising the city's strategic importance to the franchise. It complemented the existing rail portfolio and made Govia the largest rail operator in the UK in terms of passenger numbers, with about 30% of journeys taking place on one of its trains and an annual turnover of over £1.5 billion.

Govia also submitted a bid to operate trains on the London Overground, formed to operate the former Silverlink Metro services and London Underground's East London Line. Although Govia was invited to submit a "Best and Final Offer" it lost out in the final bidding process to MTR Laing.

Two sub-brands have been adopted, London Midland Express for longer-distance lines and London Midland City, which covers the network for the West Midlands, much of which operates in partnership with Centro, the West Midlands Integrated Transport Authority. The railway is a crucial feature of the West Midlands economy and over 20% of Birmingham's commuters use the train to travel to work. London Midland operates one of the more unusual services on the mainline network, the ¾-mile line linking Stourbridge Junction with Stourbridge Town on which the innovative Parry People Mover is employed.

Govia's successful bid commits it to investing over £300 million, introducing 37 new Siemens Desiro EMUs and 15 Turbostars to replace BR-era rolling stock, together with refurbishment of the rest of its fleet. In addition significant investment will be made in improving stations and introducing a new ticketing system.

The London to Birmingham route is one of the few long-distance services on which there is real choice between operators, with London Midland, Virgin Trains and Chiltern Railways all vying for custom, and London Midland has introduced a range of fares to attract custom. In addition, it has introduced a service linking Crewe and the Trent Valley communities with London, restoring a link lost many years previously and enhanced the frequency of services between Birmingham and Liverpool to every 30 minutes. The end of the moderation of competition clause, which protected Virgin trains until April 2012, will allow London Midland to develop further its express services on the West Coast main line.

In early 2010 London Midland introduced a pilot smartcard scheme in an area bounded by Kidderminster and Worcester. Although initially aimed at season ticket holders, the scheme will be extended and is intended to cover half of all passenger journeys by 2014. The card complies with the UK-wide ITSO standard, meaning that London Midland products can be loaded onto a card issued by another member, for example a concessionary bus pass issued by a local authority. It is also capable of recognising a passenger's travel patterns and providing them with offers that are appropriate to them.

In its early days there were some major challenges at London Midland largely caused by bringing together two operations with differing cultures and operating practices. This led to industrial unrest, although these matters have now been resolved. Since taking over the franchise, Govia has succeeded in turning performance around, and by early 2011 the operation was ranked the most improved train-operating company in the UK with passenger growth of 4% per year and revenue increasing by about 7%.

Perhaps the most unusual trains in the London Midland fleet are the two Parry People Movers that operate on the ¾-mile Stourbridge Town–Stourbridge Junction line. These vehicles utilise flywheel energy storage as the main source of energy to propel the vehicle, with the flywheel capturing braking energy for re-use. The first of the pair, 139001, approaches Stourbridge Junction on 3 June 2011.

Chapter 8
Diversification

By 1998 the transfer of United Kingdom's bus operations from state to private hands had largely been achieved and the privatisation of British Rail was complete. The Group therefore began to seek out new areas for growth and in February 1998 announced that it would seek to expand in new transport-related areas such as airport services and car park management.

Aviation

Ground handling covers a broad range of services, including loading and unloading cargo from freight flights, baggage handling and check-in for passenger flights, manning executive lounges and information desks, managing aircraft slots and customs clearance. Ground handling shares many of the same characteristics as bus and rail travel, such as the time-sensitive movement of millions of passengers and the need for a strong customer service focus. October 1998 saw the acquisition of Gatwick Handling Limited, the provider of passenger and cargo handling services at a number of UK airports. The acquisition also included a 50% share in Plane Handling, a Heathrow-based joint operation with Virgin Atlantic.

Further growth saw the acquisition of British Midland's ground handling business in January 2001 followed by that of Reed Aviation in August that year, and the combined operations adopted the "Aviance" brand. The "Aviance" name was also adopted by a number of associated ground handling companies overseas. Although not owned by the Group, these operations all maintained similar standards to the UK operations. The terror attacks of September 2001 reduced growth in the aviation sector,but the Group nevertheless added Virgin Atlantic's 50% stake in Plane Handling to its portfolio in August 2004. Although further expansion saw Aviance acquire British Airways' ground handling operations at Aberdeen, Edinburgh, Glasgow and Manchester under a five-year contract in 2007, this represented the final expansion of the Group's aviation services.

The aviation market is a tough one and passenger airlines face pressures ranging from spiralling fuel costs to the threat of international terrorism and potential international health scares such as bird flu. Together with the growth of no-frills airlines, this has changed the structure of the industry, making ground handling cost-conscious and competitive.

Go-Ahead built up a significant aviation ground and cargo handling business from 1999 which was re-branded Aviance. An aircraft tug is seen at Heathrow's Terminal 1. (Go-Ahead Group plc)

Meteor Parking, acquired by the Group in 2002 operated over 40,000 car parking spaces and associated transfer services for BAA. One of its best known brands was Pink Elephant Parking.

Car parking

Further diversification took place in May 2002 when the Group acquired Meteor Parking, which provided over 40,000 airport parking spaces for BAA, together with associated transfer services, as well as managing 6,000 spaces for LUL, local authorities, hospitals and shopping centres. It was considered that the acquisition would complement the ground handling business whilst allowing the Group to develop its parking portfolio at railway stations.

The parking business grew quickly with the addition of Chauffeured Parking Services. Expansion saw the development of brands including "Pink Elephant", "Park 1" and "eparking". In February 2007 Meteor acquired Nikaro, a company providing national specialist keyholding and alarm response.

In 2009 the Group decided to focus on its core rail and bus activities and as such initiated the process of disposing of both the ground handling and car parking operations. This move saw the majority of its ground handling operations at Heathrow sold to Dnata with those at other airports passing to Servisair UK Ltd although a residual contract at Heathrow was transferred to Menzies in October 2010. Meteor Parking was sold to Vinci Park Services in September 2010, whilst Securitas Mobile acquired the operations of Nikaro.

Go West Midlands

The Go-Ahead Group's emphasis has always been on providing bus services in urban areas and it was front-runner to purchase the 174-strong Gillmoss operations of Arriva Merseyside in 2001 which Arriva had been ordered to sell as a condition of acquiring Glenvale Transport. Although the acquisition would have provided it with a strong presence in Liverpool, it was felt that such a move would have diverted management attention away from bidding for the South Central rail franchise and integrating the recently acquired British Midland ground handling business. The business passed, instead, to a management buyout which sold, in turn, to Stagecoach.

In December 2005 Go-Ahead acquired the 110-strong fleet of the Birmingham Coach Company, based in Tividale, West Midlands. The acquisition, which operated as "Diamond Bus", gave the Group a foothold in the UK's second largest conurbation, where bus service provision was dominated by Travel West Midlands with over 90% of the market. In February 2006 the Group made a further acquisition in the region when it

Meteor operated a number of brands aimed at different parts of the market. An Optare Solo providing a transfer service for the business car park at Heathrow is seen passing the entrance to Park 1 which provided an executive parking service to passengers using Terminal 1.

Heathrow's Terminal 5 opened in 2008. Long-term car parking was provided by Meteor and represented the final expansion of this business under Go-Ahead ownership. An MCV bodied Dennis Dart is seen in the livery adopted for all car park shuttles at BAA airports from 2008.

bought Pro Bus, which then operated under the "People's Express" banner, having changed its name from Pete's Travel in March 2005.

Although there were some modern vehicles in the acquired fleets, they suffered from variable standards of maintenance and presentation. In an effort to introduce higher standards, a number of mid-life buses, predominantly Dennis Darts, were drafted in from other Go-Ahead fleets to improve the age profile of the fleet. A new red and white livery and "Diamond" fleetname replaced the red, white and black of Birmingham Coach Company and yellow of People's Express. Meanwhile, a reassessment of priorities saw withdrawal from National Express and local authority tendered work to concentrate on commercial urban bus operations.

The dominance of Travel West Midlands made it difficult to develop operations in the region and the way in which revenue from network card ticket sales was apportioned meant that operations continued to make losses. It was therefore decided to sell the business, a process that was completed on 3 March 2008 when it was sold to Rotala plc, whose Central Connect subsidiary already operated a number of services within the conurbation.

North America

As already noted, the Group has now decided to focus on its core business in the UK. It will, however, continue to seek opportunities for growth where these can be achieved in a way that is consistent with its overall strategy. In November 2009 it established a joint venture with Chicago-based Cook-Illinois Corporation to operated school bus services. The US school-bus market is a vast one, with over 450,000 vehicles, and has significant potential for growth. The new operation, Go-Ahead North America, secured its first contract to operate approximately 120 buses, in August 2010. As with its UK operations, local managers are empowered to deliver services in a way they see fit. This local focus and understanding of the communities it serves means that it can respond quickly to customers' needs and provide a high-quality service, delivered through continuous investment in staff and vehicles. Although it is taking a cautious approach, the Group will be looking to expand its presence in North America should suitable opportunities present themselves.

Go-Ahead acquired two west midlands based bus operations, the Birmingham Coach Company and Peoples' Express. To improve the age profile of these fleets a number of buses were transferred from other Group fleets. 497 (R461 LGH), seen in Dudley wearing the livery adopted for Go West Midlands, was new to London General.

Go-Ahead's joint venture with Cook-Illinois gives the Group a foot-hold in the vast US school bus market. (Go-Ahead Group plc)

Chapter 9

Metrobus

Success in London and the Home Counties

Metrobus operates an extensive network of services under contract to TfL as well as being the major provider of local bus services in West Sussex and east Surrey. Its high level of involvement in regulated London and deregulated environments beyond is unique.

Its origins lie in the collapse in February 1981 of Orpington & District, which had provided services linking Croydon and Orpington along routes which, despite being within Greater London, were not served by London Transport. The long-established but now defunct Cranleigh-based Tillingbourne Bus Company set up a new subsidiary, Tillingbourne (Metropolitan) Ltd in order to take over Orpington & District's services. On 24 September 1983 the business was acquired by two of its Directors and Metrobus was born, with buses carrying a blue and yellow livery based upon that of Tillingbourne. In 1983 most bus services within Greater London were still operated by London Transport, which was directly controlled by the Greater London Council (GLC). Crucially, other operators' services were not covered by the recently introduced Travelcard, which made them less attractive to passengers. The new Company managed to secure agreement for its operations to be included, thus representing its first steps towards becoming a mainstream provider of bus services within the metropolis.

In 1984 control of London Transport passed from the GLC to the Department of Transport. The renamed London Regional Transport (LRT) set up two operating subsidiaries, London Buses Ltd and London Underground Ltd, to operate services previously provided by LT. The new regime also introduced a requirement for LRT to introduce competitive tendering for bus services as a means of reducing costs, a process described in more detail in Chapter 6. Initially, the routes offered for tender were those that operated in the outer London area which, in general, were making heavy losses. Metrobus secured its first contract, for route 61, in 1986 as part of a wider tendering exercise covering most of the Orpington area. The company submitted bids based on using new double-deck buses, new lightweight single-deck buses and second-hand double-deckers. The extent to which cost was the main driver of the tendering process in its early days can be seen by the fact that the cheapest option was selected. Accordingly, Metrobus acquired thirteen ex-London Transport DMS-type Daimler Fleetlines to operate the route. Further tendering successes saw the fleet grow with the addition of a number of relatively youthful Roe-bodied Leyland Olympians that had been disposed of prematurely by West Yorkshire PTE.

Metrobus was one of the earliest private-sector operators to win tenders to operate London bus services. It assumed operation of route 61 on 16 August 1986 using 13 ex-London Transport DMS-type Daimler Fleetlines. Showing the blue and yellow livery adopted by the operator, KUC 977P is seen in October 1986. (Haydn Davies)

In 1997 Metrobus acquired South Godstone-based East Surrey. Plaxton Pointer-bodied Dennis Dart 759 (N259 PJR) was one of a number of relatively new vehicles acquired to replace much of the East Surrey fleet. Seen in Tunbridge Wells during 1998, it carries the Metrobus East Surrey fleetname used for a while.

In September 1988 Metrobus launched a network of services in Gravesend in competition with Kentish Bus, using a fleet of eight new Reebur-bodied Mercedes 709Ds. These were heavily marketed and attracted large numbers of passengers, many of whom had not previously been regular bus users. Other initiatives included a number of excursions to attractions in the south-east of England and the launch of commuter coach services from Biggin Hill to London. The impact of the Gravesend network had clearly not been lost on Kentish Bus, which made an approach to buy it out. Following agreement of terms the operation passed to Kentish Bus from January 1990.

Another significant development in 1989 was the introduction of route 358, a commercial service designed to meet requests for a direct link from points in the north of the borough of Bromley to the hospitals in the south. Initially two journeys per day were provided, using vehicles spare between the peaks on a route linking Crystal Palace with Green Street Green. Although LT fares were charged, passes were not initially accepted. The route was a considerable success and its frequency was increased to generally hourly during the week from March 1990. Further enhancements to both frequency and vehicle type occurred over the ensuing years until in 2002 the commercial operation ceased and the route was brought within the scope of the tendering regime. The route remains busy but a low bridge prevents the use of double-decker buses. It is, therefore, one of relatively few services in the capital on which 12m single-deck buses are used. The way in which the service has grown in just over two decades from a limited service using buses otherwise idle to a mainstream part of the London bus network, with a peak frequency of one bus every twelve minutes, is typical of the innovative approach of Metrobus.

During the early 1990s Metrobus continued to grow steadily, increasing its portfolio of tendered London work and adding to its commuter coach network. A number of Kent County Council tendered services were also operated. The fleet continued to be upgraded with the introduction of new all-Leyland Olympians and Lynxes together with Plaxton-bodied Dennis Darts. In 1991 the company succeeded in winning the contract to operate route 146 which had eluded it in 1985. The year also saw it acquire the coaching business of Southlands Coaches and RB Coaches of Bromley. Another local coach operator, Jason's Coaches, joined the fold the following year. Southlands was the subject of a management buyout in 1998.

Metrobus's London network grew significantly during the late 1990s as it gained contracts from other operators. Volvo Olympians with Northern Counties or East Lancs bodywork were ordered for those routes requiring double-deckers. One of the former, 859 (S859 DGX), is seen at East Croydon station on route 119, previously operated by Stagecoach's Selkent subsidiary.

Following Arriva's decision to abandon its Crawley services in March 2001 Metrobus launched a new commercial network in the town. Pending the arrival of new buses vehicles were transferred from elsewhere within the fleet and from other Go-Ahead Group operators. In the former category was Optare Excel 508 (P508 OUG), originally based at Orpington for route 358.

During 1997 the 23-vehicle business of East Surrey Buses of South Godstone was acquired. This operator had built up a large network of commercial and tendered services in west Kent and east Surrey and its acquisition marked the company's first significant foray out of the London area. The fleet was updated with an influx of MetroRiders and Dennis Darts which for a while carried "Metrobus East Surrey" fleetnames whilst the route network was revised and some services were swapped with Maidstone & District to create a more sustainable operation. The year also saw Metrobus acquire the operation of Newhaven-based Leisiurelink when that operation ceased trading. Leisiurelink had operated a number of schools contracts and a few commercial services in the Brighton area using an elderly fleet which was quickly withdrawn and replaced by eleven ex-London General Metrobuses. Following the acquisition of Brighton Blue Bus by Brighton & Hove, a number of contracts previously operated by the local authority operator in the Lewes area, together with its premises, were acquired.

Metrobus has also provided short-term cover when other operators have failed to meet their obligations. An example of this included temporary operation of central London route C1 in 1998 when London General relinquished the contract before the date for its transfer to Travel London due to staff shortages which were, at the time, a problem for many London bus operators. In August 2002, when London Easylink collapsed, Metrobus was one of a number of operators which stepped in to provide an emergency service on route 185.

During 1999 Metrobus acquired a number of low-floor Dennis Darts which had previously been operated by Limebourne. These buses were used, amongst other purposes, to displace the remaining ex-East Surrey Bedfords from the fleet. Later in the year the first low-floor double-deckers joined the fleet when 15 Dennis Tridents with East Lancs Lolyne bodywork arrived for use on route 161 which was extended to serve the (as yet unopened) North Greenwich station and Millennium Dome from 7 August. Although the contract still had some time to run,

Further expansion during 2001 saw Metrobus take over a number of services in east Surrey. New Caetano-bodied Dennis Darts and Northern Counties-bodied Volvo Olympians displaced from London service are seen at Redhill bus station in July that year.

From early 2003 TfL insisted that buses used on its tendered network must be at least 80% red. Metrobus' initial delivery of Scania/East Lancs Omnidekkas carried a short-lived scheme which tried to retain as much of the company's yellow and blue as possible. 451 (YU52 XVK) is seen in Lodge Lane, Addington.

TfL had decided that all routes serving this high-profile location should use low-floor vehicles. A contract renewal in respect of route 146 saw the first of Dennis's 8.8m Mini Pointer Darts join the fleet in the same month.

On 4 September 1999 Metrobus was acquired by the Go-Ahead Group for £3.7 million with the assumption of £10.7 million in debt. Managing Director Peter Larking, who had been one of the company's founders in 1983, said at the time that he and his fellow Director Gary Wood were attracted by Go-Ahead's offer because of its policy of allowing subsidiaries to get on with their own businesses without imposing corporate restrictions.

Further expansion in East Sussex took place on 1 November 1999 when Metrobus assumed responsibility for services between Uckfield and Eastbourne, previously provided by Stagecoach. The new route, numbered 281, was worked by Leyland Olympians based in Lewes and Godstone.

In early 2000 Metrobus acquired ten step-entrance Plaxton Pointer-bodied Darts from Isle of Man Transport and allocated them to Godstone depot. Metrobus was successful in winning the contract to operate the prestigious Gatwick Direct service, which was launched in May 2000. It provided a new link from estates to the south and west of Crawley to Gatwick Airport and was heavily supported by the then airport owner, BAA. Further expansion in West Sussex occurred in September when several council contracts for services previously operated by Arriva were won.

The opening of Croydon Tramlink in May 2000 brought many alterations to bus services in the New Addington area. Metrobus's long-established commercial service 353 was withdrawn between Addington and Croydon, with passengers expected to complete their journey by tram using the new interchange built at Addington Village. The busiest section of commercial route 354 was replaced by a new London Buses contracted route T33, whilst the remaining section of the 353, from Orpington to Addington, was also converted to a London Buses contract.

In early 2001 Arriva Southern Counties announced that it was to deregister most of its Crawley bus services. Metrobus entered discussions with both Crawley Borough Council and West Sussex County Council which resulted in a new commercial bus network being launched on 31 March. Arriva's property was acquired and its existing staff were invited to apply for positions in the new operation. No vehicles were transferred, although some buses were borrowed and operated two services on behalf of Arriva in the short term until those services also passed to Metrobus. Buses were transferred to Crawley, both from within Metrobus and from other parts of the Go-Ahead Group. New vehicles were ordered to operate the new routes, including a batch of eighteen Caetano Nimbus-bodied Dennis Darts. Metrobus was also successful in winning a number of tenders for Surrey County Council services previously operated by Arriva from its Merstham base.

The year also saw Metrobus transfer its head office from Orpington to Crawley, whilst Peter Larking stepped down as Managing Director of the company he had helped to establish. His place was taken by Alan Eatwell, who had been the Group's Engineering Director. Prior to this he had held engineering appointments within Midland Red and Southdown, before becoming part of the team which created Brighton & Hove and ultimately bought it from NBC ownership in 1987.

In October 2002 Metrobus took delivery of a new Scania OmniCity single-decker. The bus had previously been exhibited at Eurocoach Expo and carried a silver, blue and yellow livery. It initially entered service on route 246 as well as undertaking journeys on school service 664. Its arrival signalled a change in vehicle buying policy and in April 2003 the company placed the first examples of the East Lancs-bodied Scania Omnidekka into service with a London operator. They also introduced a new livery to the fleet following a decision by TfL that all buses operating on contracts awarded by it after January 2003 must be painted in a livery that was 80% red when viewed from any angle. Metrobus adopted a scheme which represented an almost literal interpretation of this requirement in order to retain as much of the company's traditional blue and yellow as possible. Whilst the resulting application, in which

Metrobus's interpretation of TfL's 80% red rule did not find favour and a revised application, in which the yellow and blue areas were restricted to a narrow strip, was soon adopted. Although a TfL contract, route 405 heads deep into Surrey.

the lower-deck window surrounds carried a band of yellow and blue, was certainly distinctive, it did not find favour and a revised scheme was quickly developed with a thin yellow and blue band beneath the lower-deck windows.

August 2003 saw the launch of Gatwick "Fastway", a £32 million public-private joint venture that brought an extensive bus priority system including guided busways to Crawley. Metrobus was one of six parties forming a public-private partnership to develop the system. It was led by West Sussex County Council with Surrey County Council, BAA Gatwick, British Airways, Crawley Borough Council and Reigate & Banstead Borough Council also providing support.

"Fastway" provides most of the benefits that could come from a light rail scheme at a fraction of the cost. Its guided sections are mainly at road junctions and enable buses to by-pass traffic queues at busy times. Whilst bus lanes alone could have achieved this, the guided sections are self-enforcing as they exclude other vehicles.

Metrobus provided a fleet of Scania OmniCity single-deckers painted in a distinctive silver and blue livery for the initial operation, a choice of vehicle which was made after consulting stakeholder groups who were asked to choose from four possible options. Unusually for services outside London they have a dual-door layout, a choice influenced in part by the preferences expressed by the focus group. "Fastway" provides a fast and reliable service 24 hours a day and within nine months of its opening over one million passengers had been carried. The initial service, linking Gatwick Airport with Crawley and Broadfield, a housing estate to the south of the town, was augmented in August 2005 by a second route. This avoided the town centre but travelled instead through Three Bridges, where it provided easy connections with main-line rail services. In May 2008 a third route was upgraded to "Fastway" status when route 100, linking Gatwick Airport with Redhill and Maidenbower, received ten new OmniCitys. These buses were shorter than those used on the first two routes and had a single door. They also lacked guidewheels, for although the new route had a number of bus priority measures, it did not have any sections of guided busway.

The first Scania OmniCity buses arrived for TfL services when a batch entered service on the busy route 358 in early 2004. Metrobus also acquired its first half-cab bus when Routemaster RML2317 was purchased from London Central. The bus, which when new was allocated to London Transport's Godstone garage, was repainted green and given a gold underlined "Metrobus" fleetname. It was often to be found operating on route 473, a seasonal service linking East Grinstead station with the Bluebell Railway at Kingscote. Despite some additional private-hire work, its cost of operation ultimately exceeded its income and it was sold to Brighton & Hove.

During the latter part of 2004 buses in the London fleet began to appear in a simplified livery of red with a blue skirt about 50cm deep separated from the red section by a thin yellow pencil line. This was in response to revised TfL specifications due to take effect from January 2005. The first vehicles to carry it were a batch of six Mini Pointer Darts which replaced the last step-entrance buses used on Metrobus's TfL services on route 336.

Metrobus operates services over the Crawley "Fastway", a combination of guided busway and other bus priority measures. On 30 August 2003 Scania OmniCity 540 (YN03 WBP) is seen on the busway in Tilgate Avenue.

During late 2004 the livery for buses in the London fleet was altered to meet revised requirements from TfL which restricted the non-red elements to a 50cm deep skirt.

On 5 March 2005 Metrobus acquired Tellings-Golden Miller's TfL work in south-east London, consisting of four mainstream routes and a network of mobility services, operated by a fleet of sixteen vehicles. The services had been operated by Crystals until August 2003. The same date also saw a temporary depot facility opened at Polhill to relieve some of the pressure on the Green Street Green premises whilst it was rebuilt. A number of other garage transfers also saw most of the non-TfL work at Godstone transferred to Crawley with all the latter's TfL work going in the opposite direction. With effect from 16 April operation of TfL route 726, linking East Croydon with Heathrow, was taken over from Tellings-Golden Miller and renumbered X26. Although somewhat shortened in recent years, this route, which had its origins in the orbital Green Line services between Gravesend and Windsor, is a challenge to operate in view of the very heavy traffic congestion in the towns through which it passes. Five single-door Scania OmniCitys were acquired to operate the service. Their arrival marked a further simplification of the livery carried by buses on TfL services as they arrived in all-over red. Whilst the livery carried by London buses was being simplified, a new provincial scheme was introduced, consisting of a light blue body with dark blue front separated by pale grey relief. An interim scheme for the remainder of the fleet saw yellow overpainted in pale blue as the relief colour. In November seven Scania Omnicitys entered service on route 1 in Crawley.

During the autumn of 2005 Metrobus was awarded the contract to operate TfL route 127 from April 2006. The incumbent operator, Centra, was experiencing a number of challenges at the time including poor labour relations and maintenance issues, and having learnt that it was to lose the contract, sought an early exit. Arrangements were therefore made for Metrobus to assume control on a temporary basis from 10 December. The route was the first to be operated from the company's new Croydon depot and the service was initially provided by a fleet of Plaxton-bodied Volvo B7TLs hired from fellow Go-Ahead company London Central. New Scania Omnidekkas were ordered and arrived during the spring of 2006 in time for the formal takeover of the contract. This period also saw the arrival of 23 of Scania's OmniTown midibus and, later in the year, a further twelve Darts with East Lancs bodywork. These had a transition styling in that they were basically to Myllennium design but had front and rear mouldings to the coachbuilder's new "Esteem" style. The Scanias were for use on TfL routes 181 and 284 which had been won on tendering from Stagecoach, whilst the Darts were to meet new contract requirements on routes 138 and 367. Further similar vehicles followed later in the year to upgrade routes 146 and 336.

Godstone garage, which had been inherited in June 1997 with the East Surrey business, closed after service on 24 February 2006 with most buses transferring to Croydon, although some vehicles and routes also moved to Crawley and Orpington. Further garage reallocations took place from 2 June when the rebuilt Green Street Green premises returned to full operation, allowing the short-term accommodation at Polhill to be vacated.

In December 2007 Metrobus acquired the TfL contracts and vehicles of First's Orpington operations. One of 35 Marshall-bodied Dennis Darts acquired with this operation, 133 (LT02 ZDC), passes along Windsor Drive, Green Street Green, a week after the transfer. These routes were successfully retained by Metrobus when re-tendered during 2011.

In June 2007 Metrobus was awarded the Surrey County Council tender for routes 409 and 411 when Southdown PSV announced that it wished to relinquish the contract it had won the previous year. These services had previously been operated by Metrobus since the spring of 2001, when the 409 was diverted away from its long-standing route via Old Coulsdon and Purley to serve Chelsham. Although most vehicles on the routes were single-deckers, there was a specific requirement for two double-deckers to meet schools commitments. Metrobus ordered two Optare Olympus-bodied Scania buses for the purpose but late delivery, caused by restructuring at the body builder, led to the order being changed to one for integral Scania OmniCity double-deckers. The new Scania buses finally arrived during July 2008 and were the first double-deckers to carry the new provincial livery. They were, however, to remain on their designated routes only for a short period as damage caused by overhanging trees led to their being transferred to other services.

Other fleet developments during the year saw two of Optare's narrow Solos enter service on route R8 which ran over a number of roads with limited clearance in the Biggin Hill area. The spring saw the first MAN products join the fleet when five MAN 12.240 buses carrying East Lancs Esteem bodies joined the fleet for use on route R2, thus allowing the vehicles acquired from Tellings-Golden Miller to be returned to their lessors. August saw the arrival of the last Scania Omnidekkas to join the fleet to a modified engine design that met Euro 4 emissions constraints.

On 8 December 2007 Metrobus acquired the Orpington operations of First London together with 35 buses, all Marshall-bodied Dennis Darts. This operation had initially been set up as Orpington Buses in December 1995 and had had a reasonable level of success in gaining contracts, most notably winning that for route 61 from Metrobus. It had, however, suffered from the loss of a considerable amount of work more recently and was physically isolated from the rest of First's London network.

Metrobus continued to gain additional TfL contracts during 2008, taking on the operation of route 293, linking Epsom and Morden, from 30 August, and the 202, between Blackheath and Crystal Palace, from 13 September. Whilst the 293 was operated with additional Scania OmniCitys the 202 was initially served by existing Omnidekkas and Darts until such time as its designated vehicles, new MCV Evolution-bodied MAN 14.240s, arrived in the spring of 2009. The arrival of these buses allowed the start of a cascade of Omnidekkas to Crawley, where they enabled the withdrawal of Olympians. Early 2009 also saw the arrival of a trio of MANs, this time with ADL Enviro200 bodywork, mainly for use on route T32.

A key aspect of Boris Johnson's campaign to be elected as Mayor of London in 2008 had been to improve orbital bus routes within the capital. On 22 November this led to a doubling of the frequency on route X26 to provide a bus every 30 minutes. In order to resource this Metrobus took, on short-term loan, five Mercedes-Benz Citaros previously

Metrobus acquired the Horsham services of Arriva in October 2009. Seen in Roffey during March 2012 is newly delivered ADL Enviro200 739 (SN12 AAU). Further similar vehicles have been delivered for use on recent TfL contract gains and retentions.

operated by Epsom Buses on route 293. These vehicles remained in the fleet until the summer of 2009 when they were replaced by Scania OmniCitys transferred from Crawley. The Scanias had been released as a result of similar new buses arriving for the "Fastway" services which are operated by vehicles less than five years old.

A notable landmark in the company's history took place on the last day of 2008 when the final bus in blue and yellow livery, Crawley-based Olympian 844, was withdrawn from service.

Metrobus enjoyed further growth in the London market during the spring of 2009 when it gained contracts to operate TfL routes 54 and 75, previously held by Selkent, for which Optare-bodied Scanias were ordered. Delays at the bodybuilders meant that these were not delivered in time for the start of the contract so Metrobus hired a number of buses from Selkent in the interim. During September further Scania OmniCity double-deckers began to arrive. These vehicles were ordered for use on route 64 but were initially employed on route 119 until the local authority had attended to low trees on their intended route.

Further retrenchment by Arriva in Surrey and West Sussex saw operations at Horsham transferred to Metrobus with effect from 3 October 2009. The network included five town services; route 93 to Dorking, TfL route 465 linking Dorking with Kingston and a handful of school and supermarket services. A series of early improvements were made including, from the first day of operation, the introduction of real-time information on all routes and next-stop displays on buses. A timetable booklet was also distributed to households in the area, whilst further enhancements included the introduction of "PlusBus" tickets for journeys within the Horsham area. Significant investment in the town's network saw six new ADL Enviro200s introduced in March 2012.

On 7 August 2010 Metrobus withdrew its last Olympians from service and its fleet became 100% low-floor. The company had a long association with the type, which started in 1985. Subsequently a total of 103 Olympians have been operated with both Leyland and Volvo-built chassis, featuring bodywork by ECW, Roe, Leyland, Northern Counties and East Lancs. Most of the final Olympians remaining in service were transferred to Go South Coast for further use on Isle of Wight schools work.

During 2011 Metrobus continued to gain TfL work and was successful in retaining those for the Orpington area network, although it lost the contracts for routes X26 and 465 during 2012. Pressure on local authority expenditure saw Surrey County Council review its tendered network in the Tandridge area during 2011. This saw a number of services previously operated under contract, including East Grinstead-Lingfield and Redhill-Caterham, registered commercially from September 2011.

Since becoming part of the Go-Ahead Group, Metrobus has grown in terms of size, profile, turnover and profitability. Its fleet, which is 100% accessible, has increased from 190 to 450 with an average age of about 5.5 years, well below the industry average. Services operated on behalf of TfL represent about 75% of its operations, with the remainder comprising a combination of commercial and county council tendered operations in Surrey and West Sussex.

Metrobus now has an official page on the social networking site Facebook, where members can become "fans" of Metrobus and access pictures, information, debates, events and videos. This facility also allows service updates to be posted, a facility that proved its worth during the adverse weather conditions experienced in the winters of 2009 and 2010. There is also a carbon-footprint calculator which allows people to compare bus and car in terms of the amount of carbon created by their journeys.

The TfL league tables, which report operator performance on a range of punctuality and reliability measures, consistently place Metrobus among their highest achievers, whilst its Crawley and Horsham town networks have been revitalised and, despite being areas with high levels of car ownership, have seen passenger numbers grow significantly as a result of delivering an attractive service. As local-authority transport budgets come under increasing pressure the company will continue to seek further growth in its commercial operations in these areas.

Chapter 10

Go South Coast

Serving the coast, cities and countryside

With a fleet size of over 600, Go South Coast is the third-largest bus operator in the Go-Ahead Group, yet the brand does not appear on any vehicles. It comprises three main bus operations, Wilts & Dorset, Southern Vectis and Bluestar together with Damory Coaches, Tourist Coaches and Marchwood Motorways. It operates in a large part of central southern England, ranging from intensive urban services in Southampton, Bournemouth and Poole to rural services both on the Isle of Wight and the mainland. An engineering operation, Hants & Dorset Trim, is also owned.

The origins of Go South Coast date back to August 2003 when Wilts & Dorset, including Damory and Tourist, was acquired by Go-Ahead for £31.6 million.

Wilts & Dorset

The Wilts & Dorset Bus Company was created in April 1983 when Hants & Dorset Motor Services was split into smaller units in advance of deregulation and privatisation. The name, however, owes its origins to Wilts & Dorset Motor Services, established in 1915 to operate services between Salisbury and Amesbury. Operations expanded to cover a large part of Wiltshire, east Dorset and, perversely, west Hampshire. Although closely linked with Southdown in its early years, by 1930 the company had become a subsidiary of Tilling & British Automobile Traction (TBAT) and the Southern Railway. It became part of Tilling Motor Services in 1942 when TBAT was wound up, and passed into state control when Tilling's transport interests were sold to the British Transport Commission in 1948.

Although pre-war Wilts & Dorset buses were predominantly Leylands, later purchases were primarily Eastern Coach Works-bodied Bristols in Tilling red-and-cream livery. The fleet grew during World War II, largely as the result of increased military activity in and around Salisbury Plain, and expansion continued in the early post-war

In post-war years the Wilts & Dorset fleet was typified by ECW-bodied Bristols. Seen in Winton Square, Basingstoke, is 803 (XMR 950), a 1961 Bristol MW6G. Services in this north Hampshire town passed to Wilts & Dorset following the sale of Red & White, and its Venture subsidiary, to the BTC in 1950. (Tony Wilson)

After privatisation Wilts & Dorset adopted a red, white and black livery. 2348 (E348 REL) was one of a number of MCW Metroriders acquired to help tackle competition in Salisbury from Badgerline. The company would go on to order further examples of the updated MetroRider after production was taken over by Optare, beginning a long association with Optare products.

period when Wilts & Dorset acquired the Basingstoke-based operations of Venture in November 1950. Further expansion took place in 1963 when Silver Star Motor Services, based in Porton Down, passed to Wilts & Dorset in what was officially described as a merger. Silver Star's fleet of 23 Leylands, including four early Atlanteans, injected some variety into the Wilts & Dorset fleet.

In April 1964 the company became a subsidiary of Hants & Dorset, although it retained a discrete identity meaning that, other than a change of legal lettering, there was little evidence of the change of control until the combined fleets were renumbered into a common sequence in September 1971. Along with the THC's other interests, Hants & Dorset became a subsidiary of the NBC from 1 January 1969.

Integration of Wilts & Dorset's operations with those of its southern neighbour was completed in March 1972 when the company, together with the still extant – but non-operational – Venture subsidiary, ceased to trade. Hants & Dorset fleetnames quickly appeared on buses and publicity, although a link to the past was maintained by the enlarged company's decision to adopt NBC red livery (Hants & Dorset buses had been green). Former Wilts & Dorset services were also renumbered to eliminate duplication by adding 200 to the previous number.

In 1983 the "new" Wilts & Dorset company assumed control of operations based in Poole, Salisbury, Ringwood, Blandford, Lymington, Pewsey and Swanage. It inherited a fleet composed largely of NBC standards such as Leyland Nationals and ECW-bodied Bristol VRTs, although variety was added by a small number of Daimler Fleetlines, including a small batch originally ordered by Provincial.

Wilts & Dorset was sold to a three-man management team, comprising Hugh Malone, Andrew Bryce and Rodney Luxton, on 24 June 1987 for £3 million. The new owners were quickly required to react to the introduction of competitive services in Salisbury by Badgerline and in the Bournemouth/Poole conurbation by Badger Vectis, a joint venture between Badgerline and Southern Vectis, both of whom had bid for the operation. The company responded to these incursions with a fleet of MCW Metrorider minibuses which were delivered in a newly adopted livery of red with white and black. A close relationship was developed with Optare which saw Wilts & Dorset take delivery of a large fleet of Spectra double-deckers, in both step-entrance and low-floor forms, making it the largest operator of the type. Significant numbers of Delta and Excel single-deckers also joined the fleet and the two companies worked closely to develop the Solo midibus. Small numbers of second-hand vehicles were also acquired, including a number of Leyland Olympians from Crosville Cymru, North Devon and Yorkshire Rider.

Wilts & Dorset was acquired by the Group in 2004. The first major initiative under new ownership was a thorough revision of services linking Bournemouth and Poole which saw the launch of the "more" brand in December that year. The initial fleet of 30 Wright-bodied Volvo B7RLEs, such as 115 (HF54 HGG), was subsequently augmented by Mercedes-Benz Citaros.

Significant investment saw 61 Scania Omnicity double-deck buses join the Go South Coast fleets during 2008/9. Wilts & Dorset 1138 (HF09 BJX) is seen in Salisbury bus station next to 3165 (W165 RFX), one of a large fleet of DAF Optare Spectras delivered prior to the company passing to Go-Ahead.

In the summer of 1998 Wilts & Dorset converted its Salisbury city services to low-floor operation with a fleet of 16 Optare Solos and three Spectras, thus making Salisbury one of the first urban areas in Britain to benefit from such an initiative.

The company made a number of acquisitions, commencing with that of Verwood Transport in February 1989. Subsequent purchases saw Blandford-based Damory Coaches and Oakfield Travel join the fold together with Stanbridge-based Stanbridge & Crichel. These operations were all transferred to a resurrected Hants & Dorset company trading as Damory Coaches. In February 1995 Figheldean-based Tourist Coaches, Levers and Kingston Coaches were also acquired. Both Damory and Tourist provide a number of services in rural areas, largely under contract to local authorities, together with their coaching operations. Although an integral part of the Tourist fleet, some vehicles continue to carry Levers, Kingston or Bell's branding for marketing purposes.

July 2004 saw the launch of Route One, an initiative supported by Poole Borough Council and housing developer Crest Nicholson as part of the Poole Quarter Residential Travel Plan. A blue livery, drawing its inspiration from that used by the erstwhile Poole Tramways, was applied to two Optare Solo midibuses. From the summer of 2009 the service was tendered by Poole Borough Council and a pair of new Optare Solo SRs were delivered in a revised livery.

During early 2004 the two remaining directors of Wilts & Dorset wished to retire and made an approach to Go-Ahead, largely because they were keen to ensure that the company's identity and local autonomy were protected, something that would have been less likely had it been sold to another of the big groups. Go-Ahead appointed its own management team, led by Alex Carter as Managing Director.

In the autumn of 2004 Wilts & Dorset secured a contract to provide services on behalf of Bournemouth University previously operated by Yellow Buses. Four Optare Spectras were repainted in a new livery of blue with a red skirt upswept at the rear, with "Unilinx" branding, for the launch of services. They were joined in early 2005 by four East Lancs-bodied Volvo B7TLs which had convertible bodywork allowing them to be used as open-toppers during the university holidays. The contract was re-awarded to Wilts & Dorset for a further five years in 2009 and a new fleet of ADL Enviro400-bodied Scania double-deckers augmented by a Wright-bodied Scania single-decker were acquired. These buses carried a new livery incorporating the university's corporate

Further investment saw 12 Optare Olympus-bodied Scanias delivered to Swanage during the summer of 2009. These buses replaced the entire fleet at that depot where services were rebranded "Purbeck Breezer". 1412 (HF09 FVT) and partial open-top 1403 (HF09 FVW) take on passengers at Swanage station shortly after delivery.

colours of white and pink together with appropriate branding. An ex-London General articulated Mercedes-Benz Citaro helps boost peak capacity.

December 2004 saw the launch of the "more" brand in Bournemouth and Poole. A fleet of 30 Wright-bodied Volvo B7RLE buses on two routes between the towns replaced the five subtly different services previously operated. The well-appointed buses, with air-conditioning and low-density seating, wore a new livery based on that used for "Unilinx". At the same time three services linking Poole with the housing estates of Canford Heath were also upgraded to "more" standards. Of the two trunk "more" services, one initially ran to Bournemouth's travel interchange whilst the other crossed the conurbation to serve Christchurch and the villages of Burton and Somerford. The former was subsequently extended to an out-of-town shopping centre at Castlepoint with a number of Mercedes-Benz Citaros augmenting the original fleet. These services represented significant competition with Yellow Buses, the sale of which had been initiated by Bournemouth Borough Council shortly before Christmas 2004. Go-Ahead submitted a bid for this business, seeking to replicate the success of the single network provided by Brighton & Hove, although this was not successful and the operation passed to the French state-owned Transdev. "more" proved to be a great success, with patronage growing by 30% in its first twelve months, and the operation won the inaugural Bus Marketing Campaign section of the 2005 UK Bus Awards. The network has been revised subtly over the years, with services east of Boscombe being withdrawn from May 2008. At the same time a night service was introduced, under a risk-sharing agreement with the local authority, on Friday and Saturday nights. During the summer of 2010 the "more" brand was refreshed, the buses being refurbished and repainted in a mid-blue livery in advance of replacement in 2012 by a new fleet.

Further service enhancements during 2005 saw additional Volvo B7s enter service from Lymington, primarily for use on routes to Bournemouth. These carried a variation on the new livery, adopted as standard, in which the red and blue areas were reversed.

In early 2006 Wilts & Dorset took delivery of 30 Mercedes-Benz Citaros. Whilst some were used on "more" services, others were allocated to Poole for use on services to Wimborne, branded as "the Wimborne Flyer", and Salisbury. Some of the latter were used on the primary city route, serving the district hospital, which was branded as "Pulseline", whilst the remainder appeared on route X4, linking Salisbury with Bath and jointly operated with First.

In February 2006 Wilts & Dorset acquired Hants & Dorset Trim Ltd, a company providing bus refurbishment and accident repair services and a seat re-trimming service to bus and coach operators, for £4.3 million. Hants &

Since its launch in December 2004 passenger numbers using Wilts & Dorset's "more" services have more than doubled. Following a refresh of the brand in 2010 further enhancements saw the original fleet replaced by 36 new Wrightbus-bodied Volvo B7RLE buses in 2012. The first of the batch, 2251 (HF12 GVP), climbs out of Bournemouth town centre shortly after delivery.

Dorset Trim, based in Eastleigh, had been established in 1986 by Peter Drew, who had been works superintendent at Hants & Dorset Engineering Ltd. In addition to providing engineering services for Go South Coast companies, the facility offers a repair and refurbishment facility both to other Go-Ahead companies and third-party operators.

During 2008/9 Go South Coast invested heavily in new Scania double-deck buses, 29 joining the Wilts & Dorset fleet. Seventeen of these are integral OmniCitys, which were allocated to Ringwood and Salisbury. They introduced a subtly updated version of the livery launched in 2004, with route branding for the services on which they operate. The remaining buses, a combination of open-top, convertible and closed top, carry bodywork to Optare's Olympus design and are allocated to Swanage depot where they replaced the entire fleet. The new fleet carries a distinctive blue and green livery and "Purbeck Breezer" branding and is used on services linking Swanage with Poole and Bournemouth – the latter crossing the mouth of Poole Harbour by way of the Sandbanks ferry. The investment in new vehicles, together with additional buses cascaded from Southern Vectis, meant that the final Bristol VRs were withdrawn from service in March 2009. Although three vehicles have been retained in the special events fleet, this represented the last use of ECW-bodied Bristols in normal service within the Go-Ahead Group.

March 2010 saw Salisbury area services relaunched under the "Salisbury Reds" brand, which was applied to the former "Pulseline" vehicles and some Dennis Dart MPDs transferred from Southern Vectis. Although it is primarily an operator of local bus services, Wilts & Dorset also fulfils Go South Coast's only National Express contracts, in respect of services from Yeovil and Salisbury to London.

The Southern Vectis fleet contained large numbers of low bridge buses until the advent of Bristol's Lodekka. Ryde Esplanade plays host to 762 (JDL 36), an ECW-bodied Bristol KSW, shortly before its withdrawal in 1969. Its body profile makes an interesting comparison with the high bridge version carried by Brighton & Hove 6443 and depicted on page 31. (Dale Tringham)

Southern Vectis

Southern Vectis, the dominant bus operator on the Isle of Wight, grew from the establishment in 1921, by Frank and Leonard Dodson, of the Vectis Bus Company. In 1929 it was acquired by the newly-established Southern Vectis Omnibus Company, a joint venture between the brothers and the Southern Railway. Frank Dodson was persuaded to retire by the Southern Railway in July 1931 and the brothers' shareholding passed to the railway, meaning that, until a half share was sold to TBAT, the company was wholly owned by the Southern Railway.

The red, blue and white livery was replaced in 1932 by apple green and cream, with dark green relief, in a similar style to that used by Southdown. The 1930s were a period of growth for the company and a number of other island operators were acquired. Although early vehicle purchases had been from a wide range of manufacturers, the Tilling influence began to manifest itself in vehicle policy and from 1937 the vast majority of orders were for ECW-bodied Bristols, although Bedford coaches were purchased. The livery was also altered to Tilling green with cream relief. In common with the rest of Tilling's bus operation, nationalisation took place in 1948. The post-war period saw significant expansion as leisure travel grew, whilst from the late 1950s further expansion occurred as the island's railway network was drastically rationalised. The growth in fleet size was accompanied by investment in other areas which included the provision of a central works in Newport, together with bus stations in order to replace on-street termini in the island's main towns.

The company became part of the National Bus Company in 1969. One of the first manifestations of the new order was the transfer of Shamrock & Rambler's coaching operations on the island to Southern Vectis, which used the Fountain Coaches brand, one of a number of island coach companies acquired by Shamrock & Rambler. Fountain remained a separate operation until 1979 when it was merged with its parent. The NBC's new corporate identity began to be applied from 1972 and the first Leyland Nationals arrived the following year.

On 7 October 1986 Southern Vectis became the fourth NBC company to be sold when it was acquired by its management team of Gary Bachelor, Alan Peeling and Stuart Linn for £1.2 million. A new holding company,

Showing the emerald-green and green-sand livery adopted at privatisation, Southern Vectis 723 (G723 XDL) was one of 19 all-Leyland Olympians delivered in 1989/90. These vehicles have now been transferred to the mainland fleets where they replaced Bristol VRTs.

From 1998 onwards Southern Vectis adopted different brands for route corridors. Displaying the "Route Rouge" livery used for buses linking Cowes and Sandown is 724 (TIL 6244).

Southern Vectis Ltd, was established with shares taken by the management team and about 80 staff members. Deregulation saw the newly independent company face competition on a number of its routes, most notably from long-established operator Seaview, which launched its RedLynx service from Ryde to Sandown. A number of long-established island operators were acquired by Southern Vectis – these included the West Wight Bus Company in early 1987 and Moss Motors of Sandown in January 1994.

The scope for growth on the island was limited and Southern Vectis quickly declared its intentions to expand initially, as already noted, by making an unsuccessful bid for Wilts & Dorset. In March 1987 it helped launch a new operation in Southampton, with the establishment of Solent Blue Line. That the new operation was a success is clear from its continuing strength as Bluestar, examined in more detail later in this section. In early 1988 Portsmouth City Council indicated that it wished to sell its arm's-length bus operation, Portsmouth City Transport Ltd, for which Southern Vectis bid £1.15 million. Following due diligence, the financial state of the operation became apparent and the offer was reduced to £700,000 whilst some of the undertakings previously given with respect to service levels and staff pensions were retracted. This prompted an adverse reaction from the council and the bid was withdrawn.

Initial orders after privatisation were for Iveco minibuses, the first of which arrived in 1987. These were followed in 1989 by the first full-size buses, all-Leyland Olympians delivered in the emerald green and greensand livery that had replaced the NBC's corporate scheme. Further Olympians, with Northern Counties bodywork, arrived in 1993 and introduced a new livery of dark green and parchment, subsequently adopted across the fleet. Similar vehicles followed, although now badged as Volvos, whilst single-deck requirements were met by more Ivecos and a batch of UVG-bodied Dennis Darts delivered in 1996/7. During this period the company was also noted for its vintage fleet, which saw a number of older vehicles used in normal service, although this operation ceased after the 1997 season.

In June 1994 Southern Vectis plc acquired a shareholding in the Polish bus company Kaliskie Linie Autobusowe, a stake that was retained until 2010 when the interest was sold to the City of Kalisz. In October 1995 it was the only former NBC subsidiary to obtain a listing on the newly-created Alternative Investments Market. This funded further acquisitions, including an environmental-services operation and a self-drive car and van hire business, although these activities have subsequently been disposed of. The company was also responsible for developing and distributing the Great Britain Bus Timetable, an attempt to provide a single UK-wide guide to bus services. Although now rendered obsolete by the advent of Traveline, it did produce a number of spin-offs including the TBC Hotline, a bus, coach and rail telephone information service. This, in turn, led to the development of a wider range of call centre activities which, at their peak, employed in the region of 100 people in an area of high unemployment. The company also developed Xephos, a multi-modal electronic timetable that was adopted by a number of local authorities. The business was sold in 2003.

Pride of the Southern Vectis fleet is 602 (CDL 699), a 1939 Bristol K5G. Affectionately named *The Old Girl*, this vehicle has been owned by the company since new and is used for private hires and other special events.

Southern Vectis also established a transport consultancy business, Réseaulutions, which provided advice on the design of effective bus networks for a number of clients in the UK, the Channel Islands and continental Europe.

Support for franchising of local bus services saw operations contracted out to M-Travel, Traditional Bus Company and The Village Bus Company. The last franchisee was The Alpha Group, which ran the Newport Town Circular although Southern Vectis resumed operation of this service from May 2001, marking the end of such arrangements. A link with this period was maintained, however, for in May 2000 Marc Morgan-Huws, who had run the Traditional Bus Company, joined Southern Vectis as its Commercial Manager.

The last Olympians, delivered in 1998, carried a light blue livery and branding for routes 7 and 7A, which linked a number of existing services to provide a round-the-island service marketed as "Island Explorer". This marked a change in strategy and the decision was taken to phase out green liveries, other than for open-top services, in favour of route-branded schemes. Overall red, with "Route Rouge" branding was adopted for services linking Cowes with Newport, Shanklin and Ventnor whilst dark blue was adopted for services using mini- and midibuses on the corridor linking Cowes with Ryde, Bembridge and Sandown. The open-top fleet, which included a 1939-delivered Bristol K, received an apple-green and cream livery based on the pre-war application; it was superseded in 2003 by a bright two-tone orange scheme.

During 2002 the first low-floor buses arrived in the fleet – these were a batch of seven Plaxton President-bodied Volvo B7TLs which carried a simplified version of the Island Explorer livery and a Dennis Dart MPD delivered in dark blue midibus livery. A further 14 MPDs, in a two-tone green livery, entered service in February 2005 although some had already been used for a short while by Solent Blue Line at Hythe.

In May 2005 it was confirmed, following press speculation, that the Go-Ahead Group was in discussion with Southern Vectis about acquiring the share capital of the business. On 26 May the Directors of Southern Vectis recommended an offer from the Group which valued the business at £13.8 million.

One of the first actions taken under Go-Ahead ownership was to establish a new network using Newport as a central hub, with most routes radiating out as spokes from it. This both simplified the network and alleviated the effects of severe traffic congestion. Although more customers had to change buses to complete their journey, the effect was mitigated by increasing frequencies on key corridors and making routes more direct. In order to emphasise the fact that services formed part of a coherent network, a new image was launched. This saw an attractive two-tone green livery applied to the fleet from April 2006, supported by complementary publicity. Open-top services were relaunched with a new "Island Breezers" brand whilst coach operations employed distinctive liveries and brands from well-established island operators acquired by Southern Vectis, including Moss Motor Tours, West Wight Bus & Coach Company and Fountain Coaches. A summer-only "Island Coaster" service was introduced in 2007, linking Ryde and Alum Bay.

The new image was accompanied by investment in new vehicles and in June 2006 a fleet of seven Mercedes-Benz Citaros entered service on route 9, the main link between Ryde and Newport. These were joined in 2008 by the first of 28 Scania OmniCity double-deckers, part of a larger order spread across the Go South Coast operation. A frequency increase on route 9 in April 2008 saw an additional two Citaros, ordered for Wilts & Dorset but hired from new to Minerva Accord for use on Uni-link Services in Southampton, join the fleet. This influx of new vehicles allowed all step-entrance buses to be withdrawn from frontline service. Many were refurbished before being transferred within Go South Coast to help replace older vehicles.

The Isle of Wight is a significant holiday destination. Following the introduction of nationwide free travel for pensioners in 2006, passenger numbers, which were already growing, increased significantly. Unfortunately, the mechanism for reimbursing operators did not allow for service frequencies to be increased in a cost-effective

Southern Vectis provides schools services under contract to Isle of Wight council, using a fleet of ex-Metrobus East Lancs-bodied Volvo Olympians carrying Moss Motors fleetnames. It also maintains the Go South Coast events fleet, which provides services for a number of festivals and other special events throughout the region. Schools-fleet 4836 (R836 MFR) provides support for the events fleet during the 2011 Isle of Wight festival.

way to meet demand. As a result services were revised during 2010 and the Citaros replaced by double-deckers, including some Scania Omnidekkas transferred form Metrobus. Further transfers saw some of the Mini Pointer Darts transferred to Wilts & Dorset, whilst a small number of Optare Solos came the other way to meet a subsequent requirement for 30-seat buses.

In October 2009 Southern Vectis introduced an innovative approach to encouraging car users to switch to public transport when it launched the 'Really Green Car Scrappage Scheme' allowing residents to swap an old car, scooter, moped or van for a ticket to use its bus network for 12 months. In return Southern Vectis pledged to scrap every vehicle it takes in, removing cheap cars from the local market and ensuring that there really is a switch from car to bus.

From the start of the school term in September 2010, Southern Vectis won a two-year contract to provide schools transport to Isle of Wight Council. In order to resource these services a number of Volvo Olympians with East Lancs and Northern Counties bodies were transferred from Metrobus and Go-Ahead London respectively. All received "Moss Motors" branding and, whilst the blue livery of the Metrobus vehicles was appropriate to their new rôle, those from London arrived in red livery and required repainting.

The company had operated "road train" services in Ryde, Sandown and Shanklin for a number of years on behalf of Isle of Wight Council. After the 2009 season the council decided to withdraw these services and sell the vehicles. As a result, for the 2011 season Southern Vectis provided a replacement service in Shanklin, on a commercial basis, using a specially converted Volvo B10B from the batch originally delivered to London General in 1993 and subsequently used in Oxford.

In April 2011 Southern Vectis and Isle of Wight Council entered into an agreement which saw Southern Vectis continue to operate its tendered routes for a reduced subsidy whilst increasing service provision on other routes and taking over the remaining Wightbus schools contracts.

The company also launched a partnership with local parishes and the council to run voluntary community bus routes to replace the current Wightbus local bus services, which saw Southern Vectis providing vehicles and driver training and the IoW Council covering running costs, removing any financial risk from the voluntary sector. The scheme was the first in the country, bringing together the resources and buses of a commercial bus operator with local community volunteer drivers to deliver services otherwise unviable to local communities. Southern Vectis also agreed to provide tourist information from its enquiry offices following the closure of Tourist Information Centres on the island.

Bluestar

As already noted, Solent Blue Line was set up by Southern Vectis in May 1987, in conjunction with two former employees of Southampton Citybus, John Chadwick and Peter Shelley. Initially operating services in competition with the local authority-owned operator on two cross-city services, the fleet comprised 16 elderly Bristol VRs in a striking yellow and blue livery, clearly differentiating them from Citybus. In addition, conductors were carried and change was given, unlike the competition.

An early opportunity for expansion occurred later in 1987 when Stagecoach approached Southern Vectis with a proposal to sell the Eastleigh and Southampton operations of its Hampshire Bus subsidiary, a deal completed on 4 October for a sum of £1.15 million. The day before, Solent Blue Line had acquired the operations of Basil Williams' Hants & Sussex operation, which increased the fleet to nearly 120 vehicles, although a review of services

Solent Blue Line's initial fleet was dominated by ECW-bodied Bristol VRTs. Many of these, including rare full-height 151 (LHG 451T), were acquired with Hampshire Bus's Southampton operations in October 1987. This particular bus had been new to Ribble.

to eliminate duplication saw it reduced to 85 from January. Whilst the Hants & Sussex fleet was quickly disposed of, the buses acquired from Hampshire Bus, largely Leyland Nationals and Bristol VRTs, were retained. The first new vehicles for the operation were five Robin Hood-bodied Iveco 49.10 minibuses from a batch then entering service on the Isle of Wight.

Solent Blue Line entered into an agreement with Marchwood Motorways, a Totton-based operator formed in 1955, to operate some local services under franchise, initially resourced by a fleet of Leyland Nationals. A marketing arrangement with Baughurst-based Whites Coaches saw vehicles operate under the Blue Line Travel banner for a while. The franchise agreement with Marchwood Motorways was further developed and saw further services, including the pioneering cross-city routes, taken on. Bishop's Waltham-based Brijan Tours also operated some services under franchise until September 2007.

Further expansion from May 1991 saw Solent Blue Line take over Southampton Citybus's service between Southampton and Winchester. Originally operated by Hants & Dorset, it had passed to Citybus via Hampshire Bus as part of a series of deals involving Stagecoach's acquisition of Portsmouth Citybus. Solent Blue Line relaunched the service with a fleet of new all-Leyland Olympians, whilst a number of minibuses, based on both Iveco and Mercedes running units, joined the fleet for local services in the Eastleigh and Hythe area. Although several additional Leyland Nationals had been acquired, the first new full-size single-deckers for Solent Blue Line, a quartet of Alexander Strider-bodied Volvo B10Bs, did not arrive until 1994. Unusual arrivals in 1995 were two East Lancs-bodied Volvo Olympians, which put in good service on the longer-distance Winchester–Southampton route, whilst 1998 saw delivery of four of the final batch of Northern Counties-bodied Olympians ordered by Southern Vectis.

The first low-floor double-deck buses, eight East Lancs-bodied Dennis Tridents, joined the fleet in 1999. These were followed by a similar number of vehicles in 2001, this time with Volvo B7TL chassis. Town services in Eastleigh benefited from the arrival of a fleet of 12 Mini Pointer Darts carrying a new aquamarine livery; these helped see off a large number of minibuses.

The summer of 2004 saw the launch of the New Forest Tour, provided on behalf of Hampshire County Council and designed to encourage visitors to leave their cars behind. The buses have a trailer which is capable of carrying bicycles.

October 2004 saw the debut of the now familiar Bluestar brand when services linking Southampton with Winchester and Fair Oak were relaunched as Bluestar 1 and 2 respectively. The low-floor double-deck fleet was repainted in an

The Bluestar brand made its debut in 2004. Unique ADL Enviro400-bodied Volvo B7TL 858 (SN56 AWX) is seen arriving in Romsey from Southampton.

Bluestar launched a refreshed image during 2009. A darker shade of blue was complemented by revised branding as depicted by 454 (HW07 CXU).

all-over blue livery with suitable branding for the new services. At the same time a simplified livery was introduced for the remainder of the fleet, of blue with orange "pencil lines". Amongst the first vehicles to carry the revised scheme were a trio of Northern Counties-bodied Volvo Olympians acquired from Go-Ahead's London Central fleet.

Solent Blue Line became part of the Go-Ahead Group along with Southern Vectis in 2005. One of the first service developments under new ownership was the launch that November of Solent Shuttle, an express coach link between Portsmouth and Southampton. The service had been provided by a number of operators in previous years, most recently by Tellings-Golden Miller. Solent Blue Line branded its two East Lancs-bodied Olympians for the service, which ran at an hourly frequency. Following reductions in local authority support the service, which was paralleled by a frequent rail service, was reduced in frequency in July 2007 before finally being withdrawn from February 2009.

In January 2006 local services in Eastleigh were relaunched under the "Red Rocket" brand, which saw the Mini Pointer Darts repainted in a two-tone red livery. A significant change took place on 8 March 2006 when the company was formally renamed Solent Blue Line Ltd. It had originally been established using the "off-the-shelf" title of Musterphantom Ltd. Ironically, the name change occurred as the fleetname began to disappear from buses as services were rebranded under the "Bluestar" banner. In the spring of 2006 services between Southampton and the waterside communities of Totton, Hythe and Langley were upgraded to Bluestar standard. An enhanced and simplified timetable was accompanied by the introduction of ten new Mercedes-Benz Citaros. Further fleet changes also saw the transfer from City of Oxford of a number of Volvo B10Bs, originally delivered to London General, which helped replace some of the older Leyland Olympians.

On 24 October 2006 Solent Blue Line (SBL) acquired Marchwood Buses. As previously noted, Marchwood already operated a number of services under a franchise agreement for Solent Blue Line, largely using a fleet of DAF single-deckers, the most recent being Wright Cadet-bodied midibuses used on services 18 and 19. The acquisition helped strengthen Solent Blue Line's presence and allowed for some rationalisation; services to the west of Southampton were transferred to operate under Marchwood's operating licence from Totton depot whilst those to the north of the city remained with Solent Blue Line and ran from Eastleigh. An unusual arrival in November 2006 was the only Volvo B7TL to carry Alexander Dennis Enviro400 bodywork.

A review of Eastleigh local services saw the "Red Rocket" brand discontinued in February 2008 in favour of a new brand, "Baby Bluestar". This was also adopted for local services in the Hythe area, and quickly applied to both the Mini Pointer Darts and a number of Optare Solos transferred from Wilts & Dorset. The same date also saw all bus operations by Solent Blue Line and Marchwood Motorways branded as "Bluestar".

From the start of the 2008/09 academic year SBL was successful in winning the contract to provide Southampton University's Uni-link service, previously operated by Enterprise (formerly Minerva Accord), together with the free CityLink service connecting Southampton station with the Town Quay. Uni-link services had been launched in 1999 to provide low-cost transport between the university's sites and residential areas favoured by students. A fleet of 18 new Scania OmniCitys, both double- and single-deck, was introduced, which replaced most of the buses previously

Solent Blue Line won the contract to operate Uni-link services on behalf of Southampton University from September 2008. A fleet of double- and single-deck Scania OmniCitys has since been augmented by Plaxton President-bodied Volvo B7TLs transferred from London fleets. 2009 (HF58 HTT) shows the dual-door layout used for buses on these services.

Go South Coast's coaching operations have now adopted a common livery. Damory 514 (YJ03 PPV) crosses Lambeth Bridge whilst undertaking a private-hire journey to London.

used. Uni-link is operated separately to SBL's Bluestar fleet and its buses carry a distinctive white and mid-blue livery whilst a dedicated brand is used for the CityLink service. One bus, a Scania Omnidekka acquired from Enterprise, carries a hybrid livery containing aspects of both Uni-link and Bluestar branding and is regarded as a spare vehicle for use by either operation. Since taking over operations, SBL has seen passenger numbers on Uni-link services increase significantly and frequencies have been increased on the core route with four ex-Go-Ahead London Plaxton President-bodied Volvo B7TLs joining the fleet.

In February 2009 Bluestar 1 was relaunched using new Scania Omnicitys in a revised, darker blue livery with starburst branding. A combination of new vehicles and strong marketing saw passenger growth of over 20% in the first year. Further improvements in early 2010 saw seven Mercedes-Benz Citaros transfer from Southern Vectis, allowing the last step-entrance buses in the fleet to be withdrawn.

Solent Blue Line was originally set up to compete with an established operator and in early 2009 it was the subject of competition itself when Eastleigh-based Black Velvet, owned by former Bluestar Managing Director Phil Stockley, launched services over part of Bluestar 2. This prompted a defensive move by Bluestar, and Beep! Bus was launched over one of Black Velvet's routes into Southampton to compete on a similar level. By early 2010, however, the two operators had effectively retreated to their original networks, thus returning to a degree of stability.

In June 2010 a restructuring saw the creation of two divisional director posts. One took responsibility for Southern Vectis, the coach fleets and the operation of the special events fleet, which has established a niche providing transport for a number of events including the Isle of Wight and Glastonbury festivals. The other rôle looks after Wilts & Dorset and Bluestar (including Uni-link).

The new structure reflected a desire to build upon growth in the low-cost and coaching units, which had recently benefited from an influx of newer vehicles together with a new livery adopted by all the operations, whilst also formalising the fact that the Bluestar and Wilts & Dorset operations were broadly similar in their markets and approach. In characteristic Go-Ahead style, however, discrete brands have been retained for the separate operations. Further evidence of the close links between Bluestar and Wilts & Dorset saw the latter rebrand its services linking Lymington, Lyndhurst and Southampton as Bluestar 6 from 27 February 2011, with five vehicles based at Lymington depot gaining Bluestar livery. This enabled the presentation of a consistent brand for buses on the high-frequency corridor between Totton and Southampton. Further service enhancements from the same date saw the frequency of Bluestar 18 increased to eight buses per hour, whilst in October services between Romsey and Eastleigh transferred from Wilts & Dorset to Bluestar.

Go South Coast was successful in gaining all of Poole Borough Council's supported bus network tendered from May 2011. To help resource the additional work three low-floor Dennis Darts were transferred from Brighton & Hove, a move which allowed Wilts & Dorset to convert all its services in the Bournemouth and Poole conurbation to low-floor operation. Further tendering success saw Go South Coast win some 80% of Dorset County Council's tendered public transport and home-to-school operations from the summer of 2011, plus a number of special educational needs contracts. In an innovative approach some of the work was sub-contracted to other operators including Ealing Community Transport. In addition, from September 2011 it was awarded Alton College's transport contract. These gains more than offset the loss in June of the contract to operate Salisbury's park-and-ride services, which Wilts & Dorset had provided since their inception in March 2001.

The area served by Go South Coast is relatively affluent with high levels of car ownership which, when combined with the area's status as a significant tourist destination, often leads to traffic congestion, especially in the summer. It is, however, projected to see significant population growth in coming years and the company is well positioned to benefit from this by ensuring that its services are seen as high-quality operations which make bus travel the mode of choice. It has also developed effective partnerships with local authorities to deliver value-for-money solutions for tendered bus work.

Chapter 11

Expansion in the West … and East

On 1 December 2009 the Go-Ahead Group completed the purchase of Plymouth Citybus, the arm's-length operator of Plymouth City Council, for £20 million.

The origins of the operator date back to 1872 when the city's first street tramway was opened by the Plymouth, Stonehouse & Devonport Tramways Company Ltd. Further expansion occurred in 1884 when the Plymouth, Devonport & District Tramways Company Ltd introduced a steam tram service although services only operated for a short period. In 1886 the Plymouth & Devonport (Extension) Tramways Company was authorised to take over the old steam system and construct some new lines. However, nothing came of that proposal and in 1890 the system passed to Plymouth Tramways Company, which showed equal failure to deliver its promises and led, in 1892, to purchase of the system by Plymouth Corporation, which started operating the network on 3 April 1893. Electrification of the network was started in 1899 and operations grew following amalgamation of Plymouth, Stonehouse and Devonport into a single borough in 1914.

Plymouth Corporation Transport Department started its first motor bus service in 1921 and, as in many cities the network quickly expanded to serve new housing developments. In January 1929 the decision was taken to replace trams and, although some consideration was given to introducing trolleybuses, it was ultimately decided to adopt motor buses. The conversion proceeded through the 1930s until, by the outbreak of war in 1939, only one tram route remained.

Plymouth suffered from heavy bombing during the war and large numbers of people were forced to move out of the city into areas served by Tilling-owned Western National. This prompted the council to seek agreement to extend services outside the city's boundary and culminated in the establishment of the Plymouth Joint Services Agreement in October 1942, which provided for co-ordinated schedules and fares with revenue, mileage and operating expenses being split 80:20 in favour of the Corporation.

The bus fleet was initially based largely upon Leyland chassis, although a small batch of Crossleys arrived during 1948. The large number of low bridges in the city's dockyard meant that the first highbridge buses did not arrive until 1952. Plymouth was an early customer for the Leyland Atlantean, the first of over 240 examples arriving in 1960. Also, unusually for a municipal operator, it took a batch of 60 Leyland Nationals between 1972 and 1974, signifying a short-term move away from double-deckers. They did not prove popular, however, and further Atlanteans were ordered. Following the end of Leyland Atlantean production three Leyland Olympians with East Lancs bodywork were delivered in 1982, followed by two Volvo Citybuses in 1985. In 1982 six Bristol LHs were acquired from Western National for use on routes serving areas outside the city. Although these buses gained standard red and cream livery, they carried Plymouth Countrybus fleetnames.

Plymouth City Transport was an enthusiastic supporter of Leyland products and an early user of the Leyland Atlantean. 187 (BDR 187B) was an MCW-bodied PDR1/1 new in 1964. (Dale Tringham)

The Citybuses were to be the last new double-deckers to join the fleet, although further second-hand vehicles of the same type arrived in 1999/2000. The advent of deregulation, however, prompted a change in policy and 85 Reeve Burgess-bodied minibuses arrived during 1985/6, replacing many of the double-deckers. They also allowed new services to be introduced which penetrated deeper into housing estates inaccessible to larger buses. The Corporation's initial livery of white and vermilion was superseded by yellow and white in the 1920s. A teak application was adopted in 1927 to be replaced, for the bus fleet, by maroon and cream in 1930. By the early 1970s red had replaced maroon, whilst the cream relief was later discontinued in favour of white. In 1982 a revised red and white style was accompanied by the introduction of Plymouth Citybus as a fleetname. Deregulation in 1986 saw a revised scheme of red, black and white adopted, although the black was replaced by grey in the early 1990s.

Deregulation saw the end of the Plymouth Joint Services Agreement and competition with Western National occurred over a number of routes within the city. Plymouth Citybus also assumed a number of Devon County Council contracts together with a commercially-operated service linking Plymouth with Liskeard, previously operated by Western National, although these services have since been discontinued. The level of competition has since died down somewhat.

Right: Plymouth City Transport's double-decker buses were all of lowbridge layout until 1952. 198 (ADR 798), a Weymann-bodied Leyland Titan TD5, is seen amidst signs of early post-war reconstruction in the city centre. (Ian Allan Library)

Below: As with many former local authority operators, Plymouth Citybus has moved away from double-deck operation in recent years. Large numbers of Leyland Atlanteans were replaced by Plaxton-bodied Dennis Darts such as 29 (T129 EFJ), which carries the red, white and grey livery adopted in the early 1990s.

Two batches of Mercedes-Benz Citaros joined the Plymouth Citybus fleet in 2005 and 2007. 87 (WJ53 HLR) is seen in St Budeaux.

New vehicle deliveries during the 1990s saw further minibuses, this time on Mercedes-Benz chassis, join the fleet together with Plaxton-bodied Dennis Darts in both step-entrance and low-floor versions. From 2003 a simplified red and white livery began to be applied to the fleet. A change in vehicle policy saw 15 Mercedes-Benz Citaros join the fleet between 2005 and 2007, whilst the requirement for smaller vehicles was met by 14 ADL Enviro200s. In July 2006 the last Leyland Atlantean was retired from service and entered preservation, whilst a significant upgrading of the double-deck fleet occurred in 2009 with the arrival of 19 East Lancs Myllennium Vyking-bodied Volvo B7TLs new to London General.

In the summer of 2010 Plymouth City Council announced that it intended to undertake a market testing exercise to ascertain the value of the company, although the council leader was at pains to stress that the operation would only be sold if a sensible offer was made.

In addition to the Go-Ahead Group, FirstGroup – which had acquired Western National, now branded as First Devon & Cornwall – and a local consortium including taxi proprietor John Preece and bus operator Target Travel expressed interest. First Devon & Cornwall, as the other dominant operator in the area, judged that any bid from it would be likely to attract the attention of the Competition Commission and therefore registered a number of additional services in direct competition with Plymouth Citybus, which prompted the latter to increase its own services on the affected routes.

Although First's move might have undermined the value of the company, the council named Go-Ahead as its preferred bidder on 13 November. Following completion of the sale Go-Ahead announced that Andrew Wickham, previously Operations Director, Go South Coast, would become Managing Director.

The acquisition brought a fleet of 191 vehicles and over 400 staff into the Go-Ahead Group and quickly led to First deregistering most of the competitive services that it had launched in the run-up to the sale. Although Go-Ahead undertook not to alter services for the first six months, the new team was anxious to bring about a more simplified network, based upon frequent services running along major corridors in place of the complex but relatively low-frequency network it inherited. The first manifestation of the new approach saw services linking Plymouth with the dormitory settlement of Plympton recast in July 2010. The new routes saw patronage increase by over 15% in four weeks. A further early change saw the end of the poorly-marketed "Super Rider" and "Super Rider Gold" brands.

Although the Plymouth Citybus fleet was relatively modern at the time of its acquisition, it was operating a large number of step-entrance buses. Under Go-Ahead ownership it has benefited from the transfer of mid-life low-floor buses from within the Group to replace early Dennis Darts and the remaining step-entrance minibuses. Amongst the first arrivals were Optare Solos from Go North East and Wright-bodied Dennis Darts from City of Oxford.

In the autumn of 2010 the company opened a new travel shop in the city's Debenhams store. This saw the first application of the company's new logo and marked the start of a refresh of its brand which culminated in the

The first double-deckers to join the fleet for some years were a batch of 19 East Lancs-bodied Volvo B7TLs new to London General. 418 (PL51 LGW) is operating from Saltash to Plymouth, a route over which there was intense competition with First in the period leading up to, and immediately after, Plymouth Citybus's sale to the Go-Ahead Group.

launch of a new livery for the bus fleet in February 2011. The new image, extended to the company's website, roadside publicity and on-bus notices. Amongst the first vehicles to carry the new scheme were 10 Plaxton President-bodied Volvo B7TLs transferred from Go-Ahead London which helped to replace the last step-entrance buses. Spring 2012 saw ten new Wrightbus-bodied Volvo B7RLE single-deckers join the fleet.

Unusually for a former local authority operator, Plymouth Citybus maintained an active coaching unit which has been continued under Go-Ahead ownership. In addition to a comprehensive range of day trips and short breaks, it offers corporate private-hire work and provides vehicles for third-party tour work. The coach unit is managed as a self-contained unit within the business, with its own management and frontline drivers. The coaching unit also runs a preserved open-top 1956 Leyland PD2.

The business operates out of a single freehold depot, in Milehouse, which is the site of a former tram depot. The premises have been modernised in recent years and house an extensive workshop facility which in addition to maintaining its own fleet has recently taken on repair and refurbishment work for other Go-Ahead companies, most notably London.

As already noted, Plymouth was extensively bombed during World War II and much of the city's rebuilding took place in the 1950s when urban planners tended to favour the motor car. The local authority is, however, supportive of public transport and sponsors the Green Travel Pass which allows participating employers to provide season tickets to their staff and recoup the cost by means of monthly salary deductions. Plymouth Citybus also makes extensive use of PayPoint to sell tickets.

The Go-Ahead Group places strong emphasis on the role its operations play in local communities. Plymouth Citybus is an active member of the city's Chamber of Commerce and also supports the local council's life skills programme for local school children. Perhaps the most innovative campaign, however, involves two buses, Dennis Dart and his friend Pippi, the subjects of a series of books written by marketing manager Sylvia Bird. The stories detail Dennis and Pippi's adventures and are aimed at encouraging young children to take an interest in bus travel. Two of the fleet have been suitably branded and visit local schools to reinforce the message.

Unusually for a local authority operator, Plymouth Citybus maintained a coaching operation which has continued to grow under Go-Ahead management. Showing the new livery applied to this operation from mid-2011 is 317 (BX11 GVP). (Plymouth Citybus)

Spring 2012 saw ten Volvo B7RLE/Wrightbus join the Plymouth Citybus fleet. Showing off the new livery launched the previous year is 105 (WA12 ACY), seen passing through Ernesettle on the city's northern outskirts. These vehicles formed part of a group-wide order which saw similar buses join the Go South Coast fleet [see page 82]

As spending cuts begin to bite it is likely that the remaining local authority-owned bus operators may be offered for sale. In December 2009 it was announced that Go-Ahead was in talks with Ipswich Borough Council about buying a stake in the council's Ipswich Buses business. The company operates 70 vehicles. Ipswich Buses had been facing a tough financial climate and the council felt that a link with Go-Ahead would bring in skilled management and economies of scale which Ipswich Buses could never achieve. In late September 2010 the council announced that, although the discussions had been amicable, it had been decided not to proceed with negotiations.

Konectbus

On 10 March 2010 the Group acquired the 44-vehicle Konectbus fleet, based in Dereham, Norfolk. Originally operating from Saham Toney, the business was established in August 1999 as Konect Coaches by three former employees of First Eastern Counties, Steve Challis, Julian Patterson and Andy Warnes, together with Mr Challis's wife Margaret. The new operation assumed a number of services previously operated by Norfolk Green. Early success in winning local-authority contracts saw the first of several Leyland Nationals join the fleet together with three Optare MetroRiders new to Go North East. A dark blue livery was adopted with a yellow and light grey skirt. Although counterintuitive, the use of light colours for lower panels helped emphasise the fledgling company's attention to vehicle presentation. In 2001 three Optare Deltas, new to Trent Barton, joined the fleet. Further similar vehicles followed together with the operator's first new buses, a pair of Optare Solos, delivered in 2002 for use on the Dereham Nipper network. The following year a decision to cease coaching activity saw the business renamed Konectbus, whilst the fleet was augmented by low-floor Optare Excels acquired from Bennetts of Gloucester and Trent Barton. The period saw retrenchment by FirstGroup in Norfolk, Konectbus quickly filling the gap with a combination of commercial services and local authority contracts.

In 2004 the company moved to a new purpose-built depot in Dereham, having outgrown its original site. The spring of 2005 saw significant expansion when Konectbus was awarded contracts to operate two of Norwich's park-and-ride routes, for which five Wrightbus-bodied DAF DB250 double-deckers and six Optare Tempo single-deckers were acquired. The park-and-ride sites each have a dedicated colour scheme, which saw four of the DAFs painted in pink livery for the Thickthorn service, whilst five of the Tempos wore lime green for use on services to Costessey. The remaining vehicles were regarded as spare buses and carried fleet livery. These services were retained on re-tendering in 2010 when the company succeeded in winning the contract for a third service to the Harford site, for which five pale blue Enviro400 double-deckers were acquired. In addition to park-and-ride services Konectbus also provides local services on main corridors into Norwich. In April 2011 council spending cuts led to a reduction in frequency on the Harford and Thickthorn services, releasing two buses, which were repainted in fleet livery. At the same time the Costessey service was revised to serve the University of East Anglia campus, in order to relieve pressure on parking at that site.

The rural nature of much of Norfolk means that there is a significant demand for schools transport, for which a pair of Leyland Olympians was acquired from Lothian Transport in 2008, replacing single-decker buses previously employed. During the spring of 2011 three Plaxton-bodied Volvo B7TLs arrived from Go-Ahead London for these services, thus making the entire fleet low-floor with the exception of a sole Leyland National retained as a heritage vehicle. Following a trial earlier in the year with a vehicle borrowed from Brighton & Hove, the autumn of 2011 saw the arrival of Mercedes-Benz Citaro articulated buses for use on services requiring a high passenger capacity.

Dereham is the largest town in Norfolk without a rail connection and in September 2009 Konectbus introduced a fast link to Norwich, the main employment and shopping centre in the region. The new service, branded "str8", ran directly along the main A47 road and its success was such that the frequency has been increased to every 30 minutes throughout the day. New Optare Tempos with leather seating were introduced. A free journey was guaranteed if the bus was delayed for more than 15 minutes, an offer later extended to other services. The use of GPS allows services to be proactively managed and has helped ensure that Konectbus is recognised as the most punctual bus operator in Norfolk. Continuing passenger growth saw five new leather-seated ADL Enviro400 double-deckers, wearing a revised livery, introduced onto the route from January 2012.

The company's emphasis on quality has not diminished and all drivers have benefited from level 2 NVQ training together with dedicated customer service training and eco driving awareness courses. Well-presented vehicles, supported by good marketing, have helped to ensure continuing growth with the increasing cost of fuel in particular encouraging more car users to switch to the bus. In addition, in 2007 Konectbus was judged Independent Bus Operator of the Year at the UK Bus Awards. This raised its profile and helped encourage Go-Ahead to approach the directors with an offer for the business.

Hedingham Omnibuses

In March 2012 the Group acquired Essex-based Hedingham Omnibuses, whose operations date back to the launch by Aubrey Letch of a bus service linking Sible Hedingham with Sudbury in 1921. The business was sold in 1960 to Donald MacGregor, who renamed it Hedingham & District Omnibuses, although a link with its past has been maintained in the "L" prefix to the vehicles' fleetnumbers.

The new owners embarked on a process of expansion by acquisition and bought a number of long-established local operators, which has led to Hedingham becoming the area's leading independent operator.

Although the fleet was originally painted blue and white, a red and cream scheme was adopted in the early 1970s. Whilst recently noted for its large fleet of Bristol VRTs, the fleet today comprises mainly low-floor vehicles, although a number of Volvo Olympians remain in use on schools services. The fleet is currently housed at five depots, Clacton, Hedingham, Kelvedon, Sudbury and Tollesbury, recognising the pattern of acquisitions over recent years. Its 80-plus buses operate on a mix of school and local authority contracts and commercial routes, both inter-urban and town services, in Clacton and Colchester.

Anglian Bus & Coach

The Group's strategy of acquiring well-managed businesses which have the potential for further development saw it purchase Suffolk-based Anglian Bus in April 2012. Established in 1981, the family-owned concern initially operated a small fleet of coaches on private-hire and schools contracts. In 1999 it was awarded a Norfolk County Council contract for services linking Diss and Great Yarmouth. Further tender successes saw it outgrow the original site at Loddon, prompting a move to Beccles in Suffolk in October 2000. The first commercial service, route 588 from Halesworth to Norwich, was introduced in 2003, with further growth taking place since, prompting a second depot to be opened in Norwich in 2004.

As with other recent acquisitions by the Group, the Anglian Bus fleet is a modern one with all local services provided by low-floor vehicles, although a few older buses are retained for schools services, with Scania and

Konectbus operates services to three of Norwich's six park-and-ride sites under contract to Norfolk County Council. That serving the Harford site, to the south of the city, is provided using ADL Enviro400 double-deckers in a two-tone blue livery.

Hedingham Omnibuses, which was acquired by Go-Ahead in March 2012, operates services across a broad swathe of north-east Essex. Seen on the long established route linking Colchester, Earl's Colne and Halstead is L340 (EU05 CLJ).

Optare products dominating. It was the first operator in the UK to place Wrightbus's Streetlite midibus into service, in November 2010. Most buses are fitted with Telematics, which helps improve fuel economy and reduce accident rates and enhance the passenger experience – this is being rolled out across the whole fleet.

Although the founders of the business, David and Christine Pursey, retired upon completion of the sale, their son Andrew remained in post as Managing Director. The brand and distinctive blue and yellow livery are also being retained.

Chambers

June 2012 saw the long established business of H C Chambers & Son of Bures, Suffolk added to the Group's growing portfolio in eastern England. Established in 1877 the business initially comprised a saddlery and livery stable in addition to its horse bus operations. Following the Great War operations grew to include a general haulage business and the introduction of motor buses. Expansion of bus services saw routes linking a number of towns including Sudbury, Colchester and Bury St Edmunds. By the 1970s the haulage operations had been wound down with operations focussed on local bus services and coach hire. In common with a number of established independent operators this period also saw a move to large single deckers in what had previously been a mixed fleet. More recent times have seen this trend reversed with large numbers of double deckers, including new Volvo Olympians and Scania N113 buses, join the fleet. The latter were, however, quickly replaced by further Olympians, this time second hand examples from London operators including London General and London Central. At the time of publication it is expected that these vehicles will be replaced by low floor buses made available by new deliveries to other Go-Ahead fleets.

Generally acknowledged as the oldest bus operator in the United Kingdom the fleet is painted in all-over dark red, this application having replaced the red and cream used in earlier years. The garage premises at Bures were not included in the sale and vehicles now operate from Hedingham's premises in nearby Sudbury.

Looking to the future, the Group's acquisition policy will remain focused on high-quality bus businesses in areas of growth, particularly in southern England. Further opportunities for expansion are likely to occur as established operators sell their businesses and, as with local authority operations, Go-Ahead's devolved approach, which allows long-established local brands to remain in place, is an attractive proposition.